№ 795

D0712104

ISBN 0-87666-989-5

Distributed in the U.S. by T.F.H. Publications, Inc., 211 West Sylvania Avenue, PO Box 427, Neptune, NJ 07753; in England by T.F.H. (Gt. Britain) Ltd., 13 Nutley Lane, Reigate, Surrey; in Canada to the pet trade by Rolf C. Hagen Ltd., 3225 Sartelon Street, Montreal 382, Quebec; in Canada to the book trade by H & L Pet Supplies, Inc., 27 Kingston Crescent, Kitchener, Ontario N28 2T6; in Southeast Asia by Y.W. Ong, 9 Lorong 36 Geylang, Singapore 14; in Australia and the South Pacific by Pet Imports Pty. Ltd., P.O. Box 149, Brookvale 2100, N.S.W. Australia; in South Africa by Valid Agencies, P.O. Box 51901, Randburg 2125 South Africa. Published by T.F.H. Publications, Inc., Ltd., the British Crown Colony of Hong Kong.

TAMING AND TRAINING
PARROTS

DR. EDWARD J. MULAWKA

Dedication

This book is dedicated to my son Anton and to all other little boys and girls. May they discover the many mysteries and joys surrounding us in Nature. May each day of their lives be a continuous source of wonder at the beauty, marvels, and enchantment to be found in all living things.

Contents

Acknowledgments

It would be difficult if not impossible to acknowledge each and every person who has in his own way made a significant contribution to this book, and there are many such people. The author is especially indebted to the countless bird fanciers who sought his advice on matters related to buying and taming parrots and who were the initial motivating source behind the decision to begin the arduous chore of making this manuscript possible. They provided the most important element of contribution—psychological support. The author particularly values the many friendships which have resulted from a common interest in parrots.

The final completion of this book, however, would not have been possible without the special assistance of various people who generously donated their time, effort, resources, and even their staffs, particularly in the filming of various pictures. The author is indebted to Richard and Sharon Favorite, owners of Favorite's Pet Center in Norwalk, California, and Linda and Ken Fenton, owners of Pet Palace in Fountain Valley, California, who unselfishly contributed many hours towards the completion of this book. The author particularly appreciates the personal friendship he has with these reputable and outstanding persons.

Special thanks are also given to Robert Branch of Garden Grove, who took time from his busy schedule to allow the author to photograph his performing Macaws between shows at the Lion Country Safari; to the Busch Bird Sanctuary of Van Nuys, California, for generously permitting the author to have photographic access to scarcer species of parrots, particularly breeding pairs generally not seen by the public; to the owners and staffs of both the Southwest Pet Center and the Animal and Pet Center, both of Santa Ana, California who were kind and generous in providing their birds and staff for photography; and to Norma and

9

Margo Robinson, owners of Feathered Friends Pet Store in Newport Beach, California who were lovely and delightful people to work with.

Thanks are also due to Dave Schuelke of Garden Grove, California who was kind enough to invite the author to his home in order to photograph part of the Schuelke collection; to Jean Broadhead of Huntington Beach, California, Keith Pendell of LaHabra, California, and to Steve Herried of Huntington Beach, California who took time from their busy schedules to bring their pets to the author's home for photography. The author appreciates their thoughtfulness and friendship.

Thanks are also due to Lindsay Salathiel of Newport Beach, Laura Gibbons of Balboa, and Sandra Platt of Long Beach, California who were kind enough to share their pets for the readers' pleasure.

Finally, but not at all least, special thanks must be given to Ruth McMillan. She was not only a source of constant encouragement when progress on the book seemed bleak at best, but she never even once chided the author when long hours at the typewriter made him testy and cantankerous and when mounds of discarded writings seemed to clutter the house from floor to ceiling. The author will always be indebted to her for her love, faith, and patience.

Preface

While our experience with parrots has been a happy one with a minimum of sicknesses and deaths, the numerous bird fanciers who had sought assistance from us in the past made us painfully aware that our success was not equally enjoyed by all. Of especially poignant significance were the numerous first time bird owners who had purchased a parrot, sometimes at extremely high prices, to find that the parrot had died within a relatively short time after purchase. Other bird fanciers sought our assistance after purchasing birds which would never become pets under the best of circumstances.

The idea for this book emerged one Sunday afternoon after a lady had brought us a pair of Mexican Double Yellow Heads for taming. On sight, it was obvious that the parrots were no longer youngsters. They were not only chronologically older birds, but they were also parrots well schooled in fearing men. After a few minutes of handling, it was also obvious that one of the pair was a hopelessly neurotic bird while the other would barely tolerate men at best, if it was tamed.

That lady was a retired school teacher who has purchased the two birds for pets. Never having had parrots before and not knowing what to look for in birds, she had had no forewarning of the birds' temperaments. Even though she had had the parrots for only a month or so, her trembling voice and the tears tugging at her eyes made it painfully obvious that she had become completely and irrevocably attached to the birds. Yet there was little I felt I could do to transform those parrots into the living embodiment of her need for genuine pets, parrots with which she could physically and emotionally relate.

It was from her unfortunate experience, then, that the seeds for this book germinated. Its purpose, simply stated, is to provide the occasional bird buyer with sufficient skills so that he can best determine what kind of bird would be best for him; to assist the occasional buyer in developing the skills needed to assess a bird's health and emotional disposition; and to provide the occasional bird buyer with the appropriate tools so that he will not only be able to maintain his parrot in good health, but to also guide him in transforming the parrot into a pet which will be loving, affectionate, and an integral member of the family.

Chapter 1
Introduction

It would be difficult to imagine a world without birds. All avian creatures bestow life to the air that surrounds us. Their presence fills the atmosphere with song, movement, and vitality. They provide substance and depth to the air around us, transforming empty space into meaning.

It would be just as difficult to imagine a world without parrots. Like all other creatures which man has taken upon himself to tame or domesticate, parrots add a distinctive quality to man's interrelationship with his world. Parrots have been participants in man's most intimate circles. As with other animals that man has taken upon himself, parrots have been both companion and witness to man's existence, evolution, and history.

Parrots amused and delighted the courts of the ancient Egyptian pharaohs, just as they were to later entertain Imperial Rome after Roman legions successfully conquered Egypt and first introduced parrots to Europe. But while parrots were intimate to the most powerful and influential circles of man's civilization, they were also companions to the poor and downtrodden.

Parrots have always been perceived as unique by the public eye. They have never failed to stir the imagination with visions of lands distant and exotic, strange, and seething with adventure and treasures beyond the wildest of imaginations. They have never failed to bring pleasure to young and old, rich and poor alike.

A parrot is unique because it has the capability of talking. It can whistle popular tunes. Its demeanor is often one portraying wisdom, profoundness, and intelligence. Its utterances often leave an impression of the wisdom of the ages.

The popular Alexandrine Parakeet *(Psittacula eupatria)* is a perennial favorite among breeders and collectors. While a colorful bird, it seldom makes a good pet.

Parrots are companions in our lonely hours. They are comedians in our moments of sadness. They are loyal when all others seem to spurn us. They are a fantasy come true.

Truly all parrots and parrot types are a wonder for they have so much to offer man. Yet they almost seem a mystery, a product of the Wizard of Oz. Even today, as this writer struggles to uncover the exact phrases which would best describe the feelings and knowledge that accrue from parrot ownership, the aura of mystery and enigma which seemingly surrounds his favorite parrot, an Amazon named Selsa, is truly puzzling. She is perched nearby, muttering to herself. Who knows what she's muttering? It's not parrot talk—screeching, squawking, incoherent. It is low-keyed. Quiet. Human-like. Almost intelligible.

How often I have wondered, just as now when the same thought entered my mind, "What is she thinking about?" Yet, every time that thought emerges, I *know* that she does not think—at least certainly not in the manner human beings understand the thinking process. Yet the thought persists and it always seems a marvel.

These kinds of feelings, impressions, and fantasies are no doubt common to us all, at least certainly to those of us who have known parrots in one way or another. Indeed, it is doubtful if anyone would really want to change our perception of parrots into a more rational view. We would rather keep parrots in the realm of mystery.

It seems that parrots have always been cloaked in mystery in the public eye. Parrots have always in the past been categorized and associated with either exceptionally rich or exceptionally eccentric individuals, people whose private lives have always seemed an enigma to most common folk. Such people were perceived as pursuing experiences and adventures often bordering on the bizarre and who surrounded themselves with the strange and wonderful. They were the kinds of people who owned Bengal tigers, boa constrictors, lions, and other exotic pets, all in keeping with the atmosphere of romance, intrigue, and adventure ascribed to them. So too did it always seem fitting that they would choose parrots as pets.

Parrots are, to remind the reader, creatures which until only recently have been uncommon as pets, even though they have been a popular form of pet in a variety of countries outside of North America.

Our perceptions of parrots are no doubt also shaped by the types of adventure movies we saw as children. The idea of a parrot . . . imagine if you will . . . a Spanish galleon laden with gold and jewels attacked by a pirate ship. As the pirates clamber aboard the galleon we see the pirate captain, a peg-legged, one-eyed ruthless pirate with a black patch over his missing eye. Showing no mercy, his cutlass is swift and accurate and defender after defender falls to a deck already covered with blood and dying men. Our scenario could never be complete without a multi-colored parrot jauntily perched on our villain's shoulder, screaming profanities at the still living defenders, uttering sarcastic condolences to the fallen and dying, and inciting our pirate to even greater terror and blood-shed.

Surely, this type of fantasy is common to most children, be they nine or ninety. It is the character of this one fantasy which distinguishes parrots from all other types of pets which we would include in our daily lives. No other pet can evoke this kind of fantasy from us. It would be difficult to imagine our pet goldfish as a hammerhead shark swimming side by side with us, defending us from a man-eating great white shark. It would be just as difficult imagining our pet Burmese cat in a scenario involving our ruthless pirate captain.

While we have many kinds of different pets, loving them and caring for them, they are, frankly speaking, common and mundane. They are taken so much for granted that they no longer excite our imagination. But parrots do. And hopefully they always will.

As more and more Americans travel abroad, and as the world becomes correspondingly smaller with each passing day, the tastes, mores, and customs of other cultures and other peoples become increasingly integrated into North American culture. We no longer merely accept the differences found in other lands; we adopt many of them as our own. Parrots are a common part of the everyday life of many countries, particularly the tropical countries. Americans have discovered the pleasures that come with parrot ownership.

This discovery has increased the popularity of parrot ownership to such an extent that the importers of exotic birds are no longer able to keep up with the demand. As parrot ownership becomes the vogue in the sense that people are no longer considering parrots the private domain of the affluent and eccentric, most people unfortunately approach the purchase of a parrot from a relative point of ignorance. Not all parrots and parrot types are like our pirate's parrot—talkative, provocative, colorful, amusing. There are often significant differences between one individual bird in a species and another bird within that same species. There are significant differences between one species and another, differences not always immediately discernible. There are virtually hundreds of different parrots and their various types to choose from. The costs can range from as low as five or six dollars to thousands of dollars.

While the matter of becoming a parrot owner may seem relatively simple—one goes to a pet store, chooses a parrot, pays for it, and lo and behold there is a talking parrot sitting on the shoulder while we practice slashing actions with our cutlass—there is really much more involved than the simple act of locating and paying if we are to avoid disappointment and even heartbreak.

As we noted above, not all parrots are the same. Not all parrots are tamable. Not all parrots are trainable. Not all parrots are affectionate. Not all parrots are talkative. And there is such a diversity of color, ability, size, and cost that to approach the purchase of a parrot with the same blaséness involved in buying a Heinz 57 dog would defeat one's purpose.

The average reader of this book is probably a person who knows little about parrots. Aside from a few parrots seen in zoos or circuses, parrots are still for most of us foreign to our everyday experiences. And while most of us have heard about people and their parrots, few of us can speak with any authority on the subject.

Strangely enough, given there are innumerable species to choose from, some of them extremely expensive, the average bird fancier sees one that strikes his fancy, buys it, and then wonders why the parrot suddenly died, or suffers disappointment because the bird fails to perform according to his expectations.

Perhaps the parrot is too big. Perhaps too small. Perhaps an intelligent bird was wanted, but the pet proved to be as clever as a stick of wood. Perhaps a talking parrot was wanted, but all that was brought home was a screecher. Perhaps an affectionate pet was the goal, and all that was purchased was an avian version of our pirate. Perhaps the parrot fell ill and died a few days after it was purchased, and perhaps the master inadvertently through ignorance assisted the parrot's departure.

While buying a parrot is a relatively simple act, it is an act which should result only from a position of knowledge, if the right choice is to be made. Considerations in determining the best type for one's household, being able to ascertain whether a parrot is healthy or not before and after the purchase, knowing how to maintain the parrot to ensure the bird's physical and emotional health, knowing how to tame the wild parrot after it has been brought home, and being capable of teaching it those tricks which will make it an amusing and personable pet are all important concerns which should be involved in any decision to buy a parrot.

By taking such considerations into account and carefully choosing one's pet, a bird fancier will arrive at a choice of parrot which will be a source of amusement, pleasurable company, and entertainment for years, if not decades, because parrots are known for their longevity.

Choosing a proper parrot should be an act of informed judgment, just as would be the case in buying an automobile or home, particularly because parrots can be very expensive, and unlike automobiles, they die. An informed choice is free from the fantasies and myths surrounding parrots. It is a careful assessment of personal needs and wants, a fundamental understanding of parrot characteristics, health concerns, potentialities, and a basic comprehension of those activities required to maintain the animal's health and inculcate within the bird those behaviors which will help it realize its various potentialities.

Just as with other types of pets, there can be no guarantees that a specific pet will perform according to its reputation and that it will always remain healthy. When we choose the pet and acquire it, we trust that our judgment is not faulty and that we are getting what we are paying for. Sometimes, we may make a poor choice through no fault of our own. But if our final decision on a given pet is made from an informed judgment, we will rarely make a poor choice.

There are no panaceas which can save us from a faulty decision, and this writer makes no pretense of offering all the solutions to all of the problems that face a parrot fancier in the purchase of the bird and in the ensuing relationship between bird and man. In preparing this book, however, the primary objective was to remove the reader from the ranks of the uninformed and to provide him with sufficient skills so that he can make informed judgments in buying the parrot and sufficient understanding so that he will be able to maintain, tame, and train his pet.

In the following chapters the kinds of concerns expressed here are explored in detail in the hope that they will benefit the first-time parrot buyer. Solutions to various kinds of problems faced by bird fanciers are offered here, but they are by no means the only solutions to problems. The observations and skills offered for the reader's consideration are experiences and techniques which the writer has found to prove themselves invaluable time and again in assisting new parrot owners with their pets.

While this book is primarily written for the first-time buyer of a larger bird, many of the experiences, insights, observations, and techniques are applicable to bird fanciers preferring smaller birds such as parakeets (often referred to as budgies or budgerigars), cockatiels or conures. Of course, it is hoped that the book will prove useful to those already familiar with the pleasures that accrue through parrot ownership.

Chapter 2
What Kind of Parrot
is Best For You?

If asked to define a bird, the average person would most probably define it in terms similar to 'a bird is a bird is a bird'. A bird is something which flies around befouling public statues and automobiles, squawks when you want to sleep, and makes a habit of begging for food in front of city hall. Some birds, of course, differ in size. Some in color. Some birds are crows, others sparrows. Some are turkeys, while others are chickens. But really, all in all, there is not too much difference between one bird or another aside from the fact that some can be eaten while others can't.

For the average person, parrots are probably defined in similar generalizations. Parrots are found in zoos and circuses. Some might hazard to venture whether a parrot can be eaten or not. But all in all, a parrot is a parrot is a parrot.

But parrots, like all other birds, differ in a variety of ways beyond what is readily and immediately discernible to the eye. Any eye can observe that birds differ in size and color, and after a few moments of observation, in the kind and quality of song and flight behavior. But in addition to these basically different mechanical and biological differences, there are substantial differences at the psychological level. These psychological differences are not always immediately observable to the casual and novice observer.

Like most other bird species, parrots differ in their response to their environment; their ability to accept and respond to commands; their tamability; their ability to readily acquire tricks and the degree of complexity of those tricks; their identification and

The cockatiel *(Nymphicus hollandicus)* is by far one of the most popular birds kept in captivity and a hookbill whose popularity is only surpassed by the budgie. Cockatiels prove to be easily tamed, develop close attachments to humans and are easy to care for. The occasional cockatiel even talks.

dependency on people; their ability to respond emotionally and affectionately to humans; their life-space requirements; their psychological equilibrium; and a host of other characteristics acting to differentiate one species from another. Of course, unlike other groups of wild birds, most parrots and parrot types are fortunately endowed with those kinds of qualities which are essential if man and beast are to interact in a harmonious manner.

In this context, therefore, some birds are noted for one or more of the various kinds of positive attributes suggested above. Some exotic birds, such as various species in the cockatoo family, readily respond to human affection by returning affection themselves, reveal an above average intelligence as compared to other birds, and easily acquire complex skills. Other species, such as the Mexican Double Yellow Head, are prized for their talkability and their silly and amusing antics. And so on.

Unfortunately, however, the mythical parrot which is ideal in all physical and psychological ways as envisioned in popular generalizations just does not exist. Each parrot species differs from another in any one or more of a variety of complex psychological and physical characteristics. Moreover, for every bird fancier, some birds will always be too big, others too small; some colorful, others drab; some adorable, others detached; some talkative and others silent. For every bird enthusiast, therefore, there is no one given bird which is an accumulation of all the most ideal characteristics. When knowledgeable bird fanciers purchase a given bird, they usually purchase it because of the specific qualities unique to that individual bird and to that specific species.

Moreover, while there are substantial differences between one genus and another, and between one species and another, there are also significant differences between one given individual and another within any given species. As a general rule of thumb, the bigger the bird, the more pronounced the individual psychological differences between members of the same species. And, conversely, the smaller the bird species, the more difficult it is to perceive individual differences—that is, to tell one bird from another in terms of behavior and personality.

As an example, at the risk of offending the sensitivities of diehard parakeet fanciers, except for learned tricks, one parakeet primarily responds to its environment in identical fashion as his fellows. His song is the same, as is his hyperactivity, his feeding behavior, the range of foods he will eat, and so on. To see and know one parakeet is, more or less, to see and know all others. In this sense a parakeet is a parakeet is a parakeet. (That is not in anyway to suggest that this writer has a bias against parakeets, for on the contrary, they are delightful pets, entertaining, and capable of being taught some tricks on a limited scale. To be trite, a few limited tricks taxing the inherent ability of a small bird are just as much a wonder and delight as the complex tricks learned by larger, more intelligent, and more capable birds.)

But if, on the other hand, we should observe the behavior of larger exotic parrots, such as the Moluccan Cockatoo for example, and excluding the tricks they have learned, the differences between one Moluccan and another become readily pronounced and discernible. While one Moluccan will act as if he would kill his master for a sweet cherry, another will take the proferred fruit in its mouth and then quietly—almost discreetly—dispose of it by dropping it over the edge of its platform; dropping it, I suppose, so that it will not otherwise clutter his living space. A third will disdainfully step away—indeed it may even jump down from its perch in order to avoid that same cherry as if it were some sort of plague.

To pursue the example, most Moluccans like to dispose of unwanted items from their cage by dropping them over the edge—a sort of out-of-sight-out-of-mind attitude. They will sometimes treat a hand in the same fashion, if they don't particularly wish to be touched at that moment for one reason or another. On a variety of occasions, various Moluccans have gently grabbed this writer's finger between their mandibles and pulled the finger and all over to the edge of the cage where, I suppose, the whole hand was somehow expected to fall away from view—again an out-of-sight-out-of-mind perspective.

One such Moluccan, a two-year-old male called Sammy, devised a special variation of the out-of-sight-out-of-mind response to people who were bothering him, particularly when he had decided he was through training for the day. He would also show his displeasure by 'getting rid' of my hand, but the variation was that he would *push* it off with his *tongue*. At no point would his mandibles touch my finger.

A second general rule is that the smaller the bird the more hyperactive its behavior, and conversely for larger birds. All small birds seem to be forever hopping either here or there, never seeming to be content to sit and contemplate their world, as if they had, proverbially speaking, 'ants in their pants.' They just can't seem to sit still, for whatever the reason. Given such a disposition, not many are content to remain perched on their master's hand or shoulder for any length of time. Moreover, when given full freedom of the house, they will fly throughout the premises leaving their droppings whenever and wherever nature may call.

The larger the bird, however, the more sedate and territorial it tends to be in captivity even when its wings remain unclipped. It is less prone to wander throughout the home, taking comfort in remaining at its place, perch or cage, being content to let life be as it is. In fact, when allowed full freedom, many larger birds are absolutely content to remain on their free-hanging perches for hours and even days on end. Some even become annoyed when audacious attempts are made to remove them from their perch. Their perch has become a familiar security blanket. And, if perched on a shoulder or arm, they can remain there hours on end, if permitted. A person can also be a comfortable security blanket!

Selsa, our pet Double Yellow Head Amazon, for example, enjoys complete freedom from early morning when her cage is opened to the late hours of the evening. As saucy and audacious as the best of Yellow Heads, she comes and goes whenever the mood strikes her. Having a hanging cage with ropes dangling from it to within a few inches from the floor, Selsa occupies herself for hours by climbing from ceiling to floor, doing all sorts of acrobatics, acting silly, scolding us, and amusing herself in her own distinctive way. On occasion, however, she decides that she is human, climbs down her rope to the floor, and then proceeds to walk about pigeon-toed as if all before her were her domain. Being part of the family, she is entitled to these occasional excursions, in which she is generally joined by Tweedy Bird and Sylvester, our cockatiels. We call this incongruous trio our 'miniature flock.' But Selsa rarely proceeds far from her cage area. Should we take her to the beach or to a swap meet, she is just as content to remain on the shoulder for several hours. Being highly territorial, happiness for Selsa is where the cage or shoulder is.

24

Most bird fanciers permit their larger exotic birds this kind of freedom for a free bird provides a great deal of color and imagination to family life. There is something warm and appealing to an uncaged bird which is not only a living part of the decor of the home acting in a constant exchange with the human occupants, but which adds beauty and spontaneity to everyday family activities.

That is not to suggest that birds, be they large or small, do not do well in limited and enclosed areas. Indeed small birds in particular, while they are avid roamers and explorers when given the opportunity, appear quite content to be caged and deprived of their absolute freedom. Larger birds, however, do best when given freedom of movement, for it is the freedom itself which encourages the bird to display its full ingenuity. It is difficult to encourage the kinds of qualities mentioned earlier when bars separate bird from man. Larger birds do not do well when confined to restricted quarters, particularly when quarters are small; and more frequently than not, because their intelligence* is more developed than smaller birds, they tend to become bored, listless, and apathetic with their caged environment, regardless of how many toys the bird has for diversion. They sometimes develop neurotic behavior, even developing destructive behaviors, such as plucking out their plumage, when their caged environment lacks challenge and interest.

As we noted earlier, when most people think of a parrot, what most frequently enters their mind is an image of a colorful bird which talks. Sometimes such generalizations become so engrained into our belief system that even when we should know better, disappointment and frustration result when we purchase a bird because of its so-called talking ability: fact is frequently blurred by fiction. The fact is that different species differ significantly in their ability to talk and in the quality and accuracy of their mimicry; some species seem to mimic human speech easily, others

---

* All birds, like all mammals, reflect a certain degree of intelligence, an intelligence limited only by the creature's instincts and drives and its environment. When a bird talks or sings, such behavior is not a reflection of intelligence, but rather is only an imitation of sounds it hears in its environment. Such behavior is not a reasoning power, as many would believe. This facet of bird behavior is more fully discussed later on.

occasionally mimic, and still others never utter even one intelligible word. The fiction is that all parrots and parrot types can be taught to talk.

The parakeet, often called the budgie, is a good example of an exotic bird which enjoys an excellent reputation based on myth and misconception. While everyone seems to know someone who knows someone who knows someone who has a parakeet which whistles 'Yankee Doodle Went to Town' flawlessly from beginning to end and which has an extraordinary vocabulary, of the thousands of budgies this writer has had the opportunity to encounter, it is only on a rare occasion that a budgie which can mimic three or four words has been actually encountered. Indeed, the fact is that budgies fare poorly, very poorly, when compared to other talking species.

Some one or two genius budgies in the distant past, I suspect, were responsible for the development of this reputation which mushroomed into a myth of phenomenal proportions which almost everyone seems to have accepted without question. Somehow these chattery, colorful little fellows have developed a reputation which surpasses the talking ability of African Greys, Yellow Heads, Mynah Birds, Cockatoos, and various other exotic birds internationally recognized as the best candidates if someone wants a bird with talking ability.

But that is not to suggest that some budgies, or other smaller parrot type birds for that matter, do not talk. Some do, but not many. And, when smaller birds do mimic human speech, since their voice boxes emit higher pitched sounds, the mimicked expression is more often than not barely recognizable. Unfortunately, too, the proud owners of such pets are usually hard-pressed to prove to others that the bird actually did say Hello!

Whatever the case, not all parrots talk, and when they do, the quality, extent and complexity of the mimicry will not only differ from species to species but from individual bird to individual bird.

As a good general rule, the larger the parrot, the greater its innate ability to approximate the original and actual sound because the larger parrots are more capable of imitating and vocalizing a wider range of pitches. It is not uncommon, therefore, for a parrot such as an African Grey to imitate the sounds of children playing in the park one minute, the gravelly voice of an

26

The African Grey Parrot *(Psittacus erithacus)* enjoys the reputation of being the world's best talking parrot. Fanciers of various Amazon species, particularly the Blue Fronted Amazon *(Amazona aestiva)* and the Yellow Fronted Amazon *(Amazona ochrocephala ochrocephala* and/or *auropalliata)* believe those species to be superior to the African Grey, however. Whatever the case, the African Grey is an excellent talker, although it is not as personable a species as many others.

The Mynah bird *(Gracula religiosa)* is not a parrot, although it is frequently mistaken for one because of its excellent talking ability and clarity of mimicry. While it is superior by far in these respects to parrots, it is generally considered an extremely "dirty" pet and one which rarely develops a close attachment to or relationship with its master. Anyone wanting a *"talking" pet* should take those factors into consideration before purchasing a Mynah bird in preference to a good talking parrot.

28

adult male the next, and the soft vocalization of a woman a few moments later.

Larger parrots and parrot types make better subjects for vocabulary teaching because of their intelligence. In this respect certainly, these birds have attained a more advanced stage of development, as compared with smaller ones. Even some parrots not particularly recognized as superior talking types, such as Red Headed Amazons, are more adept at imitating with accuracy various pitches and enunciations as compared to parakeets and cockatiels.

Therefore, if a talking bird is a bird fancier's goal, a great deal of frustration and disappointment will be avoided by restricting one's final choice to any one of a number of medium and larger sized exotic birds noted for their talking ability. But in following this rule, it should be remembered that not all species of larger exotics talk; and should a bird be chosen from one of the species enjoying a reputation for its talking ability, that does not automatically guarantee that that particular bird chosen will become an incessant talker.

As noted earlier, there is no one species which reflects all the desirable qualities one may want in a bird. Some species of birds may be excellent talkers but because of the psychological make-up characteristic of their species, they may not prove to be good companions or playmates. Mynah Birds are a good example. While their talking quality is superb and invariably guaranteed to astound and amuse everyone, their activities are limited to basically nothing more than hopping about the cage from moment to moment, making utterances of one sort or another, and within a few minutes after having had their cage cleaned, completely and disgustingly splattering the bars and floor with their droppings.

While many parrot fanciers insist on talking birds, there are numerous other bird enthusiasts who prefer to acquire a parrot which displays affectionate qualities, regardless of whether it talks or not; others are concerned about color arrangements and plumage characteristics; still others are concerned with seeking out various psychological traits of one sort or another. Whatever the case, there are virtually hundreds of different parrots and parrot types available to the American bird fancier; this variety of choice is compounded by diverse combinations of size, color, and disposition types. The final choice is limited only by particular whims, fancies, needs, and the size of one's pocketbook. It should be noted, however, that when a specific species is in high demand because it is admired for various biological and psychological traits, it is generally more expensive than its less endowed cousins.

Another important consideration for a prospective bird owner rests in the particular type of life style that his personal and business life entails. Various exotic birds can do quite well without human beings thank you. But others become extremely dependent on people. If the kind of life one leads takes him away from the home for extended periods of time and there is no one in the home to take daily care of the birds, then various types of exotic birds which display intense emotional and physical dependency on their masters must be excluded from consideration. On the other hand, various smaller exotics such as parakeets, cockatiels and conures do quite well for three or four days if left alone with an adequate supply of seeds, dried greens, and water. But even so, exceptions can occur.

While on a five-day trip to Chicago last year, for example, I left Mo Jo, our Half Moon Conure, by himself without anyone to look after him. He had an ample supply of food and water and so I did not feel he would need daily attention. When I returned the cage looked as if it had been struck by D-Day. Blood and feathers were everywhere. Since no other livestock were in the house at that time, and the cage still remained closed, I could only conclude that Mo Jo had himself been the cause of his own misfortune. Out of sheer boredom, Mo Jo had pulled his breast and tail feathers out, and from the evidence, it must have been with considerable pain and violence. On subsequent lengthy trips we made sure that a radio played softly near his cage and that a small light always shone well into the evening. Having been with humans ever since he was two months old, Mo Jo apparently couldn't stand his own company. Suffice it to say, he never abused himself again.

By their very nature, larger birds are more demanding than smaller birds. First of all, they require a diet consisting of an adequate quantity of fresh fruits and vegetables in addition to various seeds. For practical, nutritional, and general health reasons it is not advisable to leave such birds for extended periods of time without adequate care given their dietary needs. Secondly, many types of larger exotics, particularly those that were hand-raised from infancy, thrive on emotional and physical contact with people. For many such birds, the absence of human contact is akin to emotional deprivation with all of its consequences.

There are some final considerations which may determine the final choice of parrot species. Since birds are considerably cleaner than dogs or cats to the extent, anyway, that their droppings do not stain carpets and clothes, that droppings are relatively odor-free and that birds rarely act as hosts for parasites such as fleas, apartment block owners generally permit tenants to maintain birds as pets. Birds seem to be excellent candidates for apartment life except for the fact that some species tend to be exceptionally noisy. Even small birds such as canaries, cockatiels, or budgies can have powerful enough lungs, but their daily vocal exercises are rarely overly obnoxious to the ear.

The Amazons and various other larger parrots, however, have loud raspy voices which, when given full vent, are loud enough to seriously annoy even the most tolerant of neighbors, regardless of how cute and charming they may be during all those other times when they amuse the neighborhood with their mimicry. While birds are noisiest at sunrise and sunset, they have the unconscionable habit of screaming their loudest at the most unexpected times and generally at the most inopportune occasions. These solo singing periods or better still screaming jags, depending on one's perspective, can range from just a few minutes to half an hour or more per session.

Selsa, our Mexican Double Yellow Head, embarks on these screaming rampages not just at sunrise, not just at sunset, but whenever she wants to greet someone because she has heard the door open. A simple hello would be enough, but a half hour of shrieked greeting . . . ? We have learned to handle these episodes calmly by putting her on a perch and then locking her in a darkened bathroom for a short while. The only other viable alternative may be to wring her neck and concoct some sort of expensive parrot fricassee—a type of retribution which has been considered from time to time during my weaker moments.

Some larger exotics pretend they are in jungles and during the still hours of the night will decide to scream. Such screaming birds are not guaranteed to win friends and influence enemies. Obviously residence in an apartment complex can become complicated at best and terminal at worst after a pet bird finishes his jungle-call practice.

Most parrots rapidly adapt to captivity and become gentle pets. But some individual birds can never be truly trusted under the best of conditions. Irascible and unpredictable, they may bite a hand offered in friendship. A family with young children, particularly preschoolers, may wish to reconsider the size of the bird particularly if the species is known to be unpredictable. Small birds may be more appropriate for such children, for they are easily tamed, predictable most of the time, and less prone to inflict a serious bite should they get up off the wrong side of the branch so to speak.

If a larger bird is still preferred, careful shopping will result in an exotic parrot which has a pleasant and easygoing disposition. It is best to look for a bird already tamed, and while such birds normally command a higher premium, they are generally worth this added cost, considering that there is no risk that the bird you purchase will turn out to be incorrigibly untamable and predisposed to bite. A bird already tamed can bring peace of mind to parents interested in allowing their children to have the opportunity to enjoy a pet parrot.

Cost is another important consideration. There are charming, attractive, and suitable exotic birds for every pocketbook, regardless of budget. Bird prices are frequently determined by popular demand, and sales of birds are often faddish, with one species or another being popular over a given period of time only to fade into relative obscurity at a later date when another species becomes the vogue. For example, recently in Mission Viejo, California, Scarlet Macaws were such status symbols that there were seventeen such birds in one city block alone.

By now it should be obvious to the reader that there are no iron-clad rules to guide the bird buyer in locating a bird which will fulfill every expectation.

Odds, however, can be increased in favor of the buyer. By knowing what charateristics would be best to suit one's own and family needs and being able to compromise on various physical and psychological traits, the bird fancier can reduce the range of total possible selection to a handful, if not one or two species. Younger

When you have a member of the parrot family as a pet, you can usual-ly count on having the bird with you for a long time, provided the bird receives proper care. These birds have long life expectancies.

specimens are preferable to older ones. Birds with a given reputation for a certain quality and disposition are preferable to those species not noted for the same traits in the vain hope that the bird will somehow acquire that trait or disposition. They rarely do. Birds hand-fed are preferable to birds which have been fed and reared by their natural mothers.[*]

As with most household cats and dogs, most exotic birds can become participating members in family life. They add joy, pleasure, and companionship without demanding too much in return. But harmony between pet and master is contingent on the master's needs, personal constraints and attitudes, and his recognition of a bird's particular qualities and characteristics. By carefully considering these kinds of concerns, the bird fancier will finally decide and arrive at a choice of bird which will become an active member of family life.

Buyer beware: Many so called hand-fed birds commanding premium prices are nothing more than young fledglings taken from a nest during their weaning period. A later chapter deals exhaustively with baby birds, and it is recommended that the buyer read it should he be considering a hand-fed baby.

Chapter 3
The Quarantine Station:
Some Facts To Consider

If asked to explain the term 'quarantine station,' the average bird fancier will most probably define it as some type of facility where an animal has been confined to control, and perhaps even eradicate, whatever diseases it may have. Frequently, especially for those of us born before World War II, the idea of a quarantine assumes special meanings which reflect personal experiences we underwent during our childhood. Those were the days when chicken pox, scarlet fever, ring worm, mumps, and similar childhood diseases rampaged through large populations of school-aged children on an annual basis, as regular as clockwork, and which sometimes infected such significant numbers of children that classrooms were virtually emptied. Infected children were quarantined in their homes for specific periods of time during which no other children were allowed contact with them.

For those of us who were quarantined, or who knew someone who was, the end of a quarantine period signified not only the end of a vacation, but also some type of proclamation to the world that the infected person was now 'cleansed,' purified if you will, that he was somehow more fit and to re-enter the world of the uncontaminated.

In a similar way, I suspect, the average fancier of exotic birds has the idea that a quarantine station has endowed the bird with a mystical aura of purity and cleanliness, and has an impression that the quarantine process has transformed the bird into a supermortal being free of bacteria, viruses, and heaven only knows what all else that could affect the future well-being of the bird, or its owner. Such a bird is better than other birds, a "my father is bigger than your father" philosophy.

Lories are hardy birds with amusing personalities, but they are usual-ly kept as aviary birds rather than as pets. This is a Black Lory *(Chalcopsitta atra atra).*

Right:
This Amazon is one
of the subspecies of
*Amazona
ochrocephala.*
Below: The gentle,
colorful Scarlet
Macaw *(Ara macao)* is
always a favorite of
parrot fanciers.

In reality, however, a quarantine station is not a facility designed to reduce and eliminate disease in livestock, although it is often used for that purpose. When we consider the importation of exotic species of birds and the possible long-term effects of such importation, the fundamental purpose of quarantining livestock becomes immediately clear: the incarceration of livestock in quarantine facilities for specific periods of time is designed to prevent newly imported birds from being circulated among bird fanciers until the U.S. Department of Agriculture can ascertain whether or not those birds carry exotic forms of various diseases such as Newcastle disease or any other viral or bacterial disease that can prove to be deadly to wild and domesticated birds already in the country. Quarantined birds are therefore allowed only conditional entry into the country.

The quarantine period, lasting a minimum of thirty days, is the minimal amount of time needed to detect those kinds of deadly diseases which can critically decimate flocks of domestic and wild birds. Newcastle disease is the most dreaded of them. Should the imported birds prove to be diseased, they must either be destroyed or exported out of the country; should they be free of dangerous diseases, their conditional status is removed and they are then allowed full entry and eventual distribution to bird fanciers. When imported birds are eventually allowed unconditional entry, all that is implied is that the birds are free of those kinds of diseases which would be difficult to control should they infect domestic birds—nothing more. Sorry!

While the quarantining of birds may seem like an infringement of a person's basic rights to purchase whatever kind of bird he desires whenever he wishes, the laws pertaining to the quarantining of birds resulted from a tragic and expensive experience. Somewhere between 1970-71, a new strain of Newcastle disease was introduced into southern California by what is generally suspected to be a parrot brought into the country from either Mexico or Central America. The epidemic was for the most part contained to California, but in order to eradicate the disease approximately 12,000,000 birds had to be destroyed at a cost of $28,000,000. The epidemic was not fully under control until 1973.

It should be noted that these figures do not account for the losses suffered by various groups of wild birds such as waterfowl, songbirds, seabirds, and so on.

With rare exceptions, if any, veterinary health authorities throughout the world take great precautions and care to ensure the prevention and control of livestock diseases. But any bird-importing country cannot be fully assured that the kinds of precautions and safeguards it exercises in protecting the health of its own livestock are the kinds of programs pursued by exporting nations. For that reason, or until an international agency can be organized to coordinate international control of livestock diseases much in the same way as the U.N. has received world-wide support and cooperation in controlling smallpox, then the United States will require the quarantining of imported bird stocks.

When quarantined birds are eventually released and finally distributed among pet shops and bird fanciers, there is an assurance that the most virulent diseases will not contaminate stocks of birds already in the country. Such assurances are comforting, particularly when one already has several birds and is considering the purchase of others. That does not mean, however, that the birds already in one's collection will not be infected by those diseases that they have not yet been exposed to when the newly released birds from quarantine are introduced to the group; and it does not mean that the new bird will not be infected by diseases through exposure to birds already in the collection. In fact, anyone who already owns birds will segregate a newly released bird for at least two or three weeks until it is definite that the new import does not manifest any virulent disease which may infect the others.

Since exotic birds have to be quarantined under existing laws, quarantine stations serve a vital function in supplying the pet industry with sufficient stocks of birds to meet consumer demands. The variety and availability of exotic birds at any given time, however, are governed by the laws of supply and demand. These basic economic laws, moreover, are tempered by various conservation legislations governing the harvesting and over-exploitation of various bird stocks. Some countries prohibit the exportation of exotic birds while others place such rigid constraints on exportation that importation is unprofitable. Additionally, various legislations by the United States such as the Endangered Species Act prohibit the importation of various foreign exotics even when

The Blue Crowned Hanging Parrot *(Loriculus galgulus)* is seldom encountered in the United States, although it is common in the wild
throughout Malaysia, Sumatra and Borneo.

The Vernal Hanging Parrot *(Loriculus vernalis)* is another species rarely encountered in the United States aside from the occasional hobbyist's aviary. As with the Blue Crowned Hanging Parrot, this species is quite unusual, for when sleeping it hangs upside down.

These birds are waiting to be picked up from an importing facility. The cages on which the Amazon parrot and Mynah bird are standing are importation cages for softbilled birds.

their exportation is permitted under the laws of the exporting country.

An importer's decision to import a given species will be for the most part determined by these considerations. But others play a significant role in shaping decisions as to what specific species will be selected for importation and how many will be imported. Some species do not transport well, and heavy death rates are incurred as a result of stress. Other species do not do well in captivity. Some exotic birds can be bred in captivity, and domestic breeding programs may make importation unprofitable. Young birds are preferable to older birds, but baby birds which have not yet learned to feed themselves incur considerable labor costs when they have to be hand-fed; yet some countries prohibit the exportation of baby birds; in turn, the demand for younger birds and the fact that nesting periods differ from species to species and from hemisphere to hemisphere mean that the market place fluctuates from a glut of birds at one time to a scarcity of birds another. And then, of course, the general popularity of a species is often *faddish* and the desirability of a given species may fluctuate dramatically, forcing an importer to frequently import birds on the speculation that he will be able to sell them.

Whatever the case, once the importer has decided upon the species of birds to be imported, he files an application for an import permit from the U.S.D.A. Once the permit has been issued, or its issuance is pending, a commercial arrangement is made with a livestock broker in the exporting nation.

When the birds arrive, generally by aircraft in order to minimize mortality rates as a result of stress from handling, great care is exercised to prevent the introduction of new diseases to both wild and domestic bird stocks.

The aircraft compartment holding the birds, platforms, and various conveyance vehicles coming into contact with the birds may be fumigated. Every effort is made to ensure that the environment, materials, and personnel remain free of possible contamination by serious avian diseases.

Once the birds are in quarantine, additional precautions are instituted. Rigid Federal guidelines define the layout of the station. Besides specifying the kinds of building materials to be used in its construction and the types of drainage and waste disposal systems

43

Fig Parrots are small parrots with lively personalities, but unfortunately they are rare in captivity. This is a pair of Orange Breasted Fig Parrots *(Opopsitta gulielmiterti suavissima)*; the more colorful bird is the male.

Opposite:
The Eastern Rosella *(Platycercus eximius)* is one of eight species in its genus, all of them common to Australia. This species is rarely encountered outside of Australia due to that country's ban on the exportation of native birds.

needed in order to ensure that contamination does not leave the station, strict procedures are established governing personnel entering and leaving the station.

For example, every station must contain an office, two separate dressing rooms, a shower, and the bird housing area. The main entrance to the building must open into an office where all records—with immediate availability to U.S.D.A. inspectors—are kept. (There may be other entrances and exits serving as emergency fire escape routes and entrances for the loading/unloading of birds, but they are government-sealed once the birds are in quarantine.)

The only entrance to the quarantined birds is through that office—a doorway leads directly to a dressing room where the workers undress; another door from that dressing room leads to an enclosed shower facility, where each worker must shower completely, thoroughly scrubbing his nails and shampooing his hair. The worker then steps through yet another doorway in the shower facility which leads into still another dressing room where he dons his work clothing. A final doorway from that last dressing room leads to the area holding the birds.

In leaving the quarantine station, regardless of reason, the whole procedure is reversed. Finally, feed, medicines, and various items needed in the maintenance of the quarantined birds may be introduced into the bird housing area, but nothing may leave the premises until the birds are given their final unconditional release.

To enforce these safety precautions, a U.S.D.A. inspector remains in the office from the time the first worker reports to work until the last person leaves at the end of the day. Indeed, precautions are so strict that during those times when no one is scheduled to be working in the facility, the one entrance leading into the showers is sealed with a government seal. No one can enter that facility without the seal being first removed by an agent of the U.S.D.A.; there are severe penalties for anyone tampering with or removing that seal during the absence of a government agent.

The birds must remain quarantined for a minimum of thirty days. During that period all dead birds must be preserved in a deep freezer and are subject to autopsy at the officer's discretion. Only when there is absolute certainty that the birds are free of serious and deadly diseases does the U.S.D.A. provide the importer with release documentation. (The birds are usually quarantined longer than the minimal requirement, however, for by the time the final autopsies are conducted on dead birds and the release papers delivered to the importer, an additional week or two may have passed.)

Birds Just Released From Quarantine Can Be A Poor Choice For Pets

The procedures discussed above have a two-fold effect: they protect domestic and wild bird flocks from possible epidemics as a result of the introduction of exotic diseases; secondly, they also basically ensure that the imported birds are not contaminated by diseases which may be prevalent in the domestic avian flocks. Since frequent and exhaustive tests are taken to protect domestic stocks before final release papers are issued—particularly when there is an excessive mortality rate among imported birds—pet dealers and bird fanciers alike can rest assured that the possibility of the introduction of deadly, epidemic-type diseases by the newly released birds is highly unlikely. But a bird just recently released from quarantine is not necessarily a specimen which will prove to be healthy and live to a ripe old age, so it may therefore be no choice selection.

On the contrary, the imported bird comes from another region of the world—generally far removed from the United States—where the various strains of diseases affecting our birds are generally unknown. Since quarantined birds have had little opportunity to come into contact with domestic diseases before their release, upon their release they have had little or no opportunity to prove their lack of susceptibility and/or immunity to those diseases which plague domestic birds. Fresh out of quarantine, they may fall victim to any one of a number of diseases which plague the avian industry. While most newly released birds prove to be healthy pets when they clear quarantine, many others become sick and die.

Frequently, far too frequently, one hears of a proud new owner of an expensive exotic bird who has had it for only a few days or

This beautiful Blue Eyed Cockatoo *(Cacatua ophthalmica)* is from the Bismarck Archipelago northeast of Papua New Guinea. Similar to most cockatoos, it proves to be a gentle, affectionate pet. Due to the limited size of its habitat and its relatively small population, the species is not often available to the pet trade.

Opposite:
The Galah *(Eolophus roseicapillus)* is an attractive bird seldom encountered in North America, although some are bred from the few birds which were imported prior to the Australian ban on exportation. The Galah, according to Australian reports, makes an excellent pet, but at times it is shot in its native land because it damages grain crops.

weeks and found that it suddenly became listless, stopped eating, and before the owner had the opportunity to adequately assess the bird's health, the bird was lost. The onslaught of diseases is usually swift. While these kinds of tragic histories can even happen to a recently acquired bird which was domestically bred, they are for the most part tragedies occurring to birds recently released from quarantine.

Unfortunately, the pet industry has never taken upon itself to survey the numbers and kinds of birds lost to pet owners when such exotic birds were subject to importation and quarantining. Certainly many such losses are due to owner ignorance, negligence, maltreatment, and inadequate care. But as a result of this author's trading and retailing experience with exotic birds, the losses suffered by competent and knowledgeable bird fanciers would suggest that the percentage of sickness and loss of newly released birds is significantly high—perhaps as high as one out of three birds. And, while the death of a prized pet is a serious enough matter, the loss is compounded by the expense of the bird, which is often a sizable investment.

There is no way of fully protecting oneself from purchasing a bird which will fall prey to a disease that it has never before had contact with. When a new stock of birds of a particular species is just released from quarantine, the prospective buyer could wait for a month or two as a precautionary measure before making the purchase. In waiting, however, he may find that the birds have either been sold or the price has risen as a result of diminished available stocks.

There are not many options available for a buyer set on a specific species in high demand and short supply when such birds are just released from quarantine. Since exotic birds are always the least expensive during the first two or three weeks when they are first entering the market, it is best to buy at that time in order to realize savings. Some highly conscientious pet farms, pet shops, and quarantine station operators provide various types of guarantees against the loss of their birds should they fall ill and die just after release from quarantine. Most, however, do not.

Unless the buyer is definitely set on a specific species which is always in short supply, it would be more prudent to choose another species, thereby avoiding risks possible with a newly released bird. In either case, if the buyer's heart is set on a given bird, the purchase should be made from a reputable dealer who is known for selling only the best of stock and who is recognized for his willingness to meet customers at least halfway in dealing with problems resulting from losses. The buyer will find that these kinds of pet brokers normally price their birds higher than their competitors; the profit margin on all livestock sales must be high enough in order for the dealer to be able to offer a provision for compensation to customers who may suffer financial losses as a result of their bird's death and who can show a justifiable cause for complaint.

Unfortunately, however, many bird fanciers are not prepared to pay this higher price as an insurance policy. They may be impulsive in their buying habits or of such character that their purchases are governed only by the competitiveness of the price. In both cases, such buyers fall prey by virtue of ignorance and penuriousness to the normal lot of those who shop by price alone.

Quarantine stations, like all other businesses, are involved in a profit and loss struggle. And, like all other businesses, they often suffer losses over which they have no control. Mortality rates begin from the first moment of arrival when it is automatically assumed that birds will have died in transit. Regardless of how scrupulous the exporter and transportation agencies may be in protecting the birds, it is a rare occasion indeed when there are no deaths. And, depending on the financial agreement between importer and exporter, losses of birds incurred through shipping often become the liability of the importer. Then there is the prospect that the importer may either have his birds destroyed or have the entire shipment reexported out of the United States because of disease. Even where such contingencies and losses may be compensated for by the exporter, the importer suffers a financial loss because money and facilities have been tied up, labor costs have been incurred, money has been spent on medicines and feed, and so on.

On the average, from the first moment of arrival to the time the last bird has been sold by the quarantine operator, a ten to fifteen percent mortality rate would be considered low. Maintenance of losses to those levels does not imply that all the surviving birds are in excellent health and that only the fittest have survived. Some

Left: The Yellow Tailed Black Cockatoo *(Calyptorhynchus funereus funereus)* has a tendency to be shy. Like the other black cockatoos, it is an expensive bird, mainly because it is rarely available from its native Australia. **Right:** The White Tailed Black Cockatoo *(Calyptorhynchus funereus baudinii)* is not especially popular as a cage bird, primarily because of its general unattractiveness. While the White Tailed is considered by most ornithologists as beneficial to farmers, it has on occasion been declared a pest by some state governments in Australia and bounties have been paid for each bird shot.

Opposite:
This majestic grayish Black Palm Cockatoo *(Probosciger aterrimus)* is common to the north-eastern part of Australia and in Papua New Guinea. This species does not do well in captivity because of its highly specialized diet. It is extremely rare outside of its natural habitat.

birds will become sick just because they become sick, like all other living beings; others become ill regardless of the precautions taken to protect the birds from illness, the balanced diets given them, and medical treatment; others become intimidated by constant contact with humans because they are still wild, becoming stressed to the point that they refuse to eat, thereby weakening bodily resistance and rapidly becoming emaciated; others find it difficult to adjust to the new kinds of foods prepared for them and as a result develop digestive problems. Finally, because it is unprofitable to import a few birds at a time, importers will import several hundred of a species. Often cramped several to a marginally sized cage, the birds fight amongst themselves, adding to the stress factor. Grooming and preening opportunities diminish with added stress and crowding, and the weaker and smaller birds have limited opportunity to obtain their fair share of feed and water.

Whatever the case, many of the quarantined birds become ill and others become dilapidated looking, regardless of how low the mortality rate is kept. Such birds are generally less desirable as pets. That does not suppose that such birds will not recover their good health and/or improve their appearance given the proper conditions. In the majority of cases, all that is required for these less than prime birds is loving care, good food, freedom from molestation, and time. Nevertheless, quarantine operators have considerable difficulty finding buyers for these second-rate birds.

On the other hand, birds which are prime in appearance and health will be quickly purchased by jobbers, pet shops, and bird fanciers, while the less than prime birds will be for the most part unmarketable at the prevailing market price. If the importer is to recover his investment, he must also sell those birds which are less than desirable.

In order to dispose of these birds they are usually sold far below the cost of prime birds, and are normally sold to a jobber on an 'as is' basis. The birds are then 'dumped' on the public at 'bargain' prices with the full knowledge that many of the birds will not be surviving a month or two later. The unsuspecting customer is never informed that the bird is suffering health problems.

Let's be candid. The average potential bird buyer is, unfortunately, a person with a limited knowledge of exotic birds. His familiarity with birds is limited to a few brief exposures in zoos or through television programs. At best, he is familiar with someone who already owns a parrot. As such, his knowledge of bird health and bird care is severely handicapped to say the least.

As most pet shop owners will testify, a significant proportion of bird sales results from impulse buying habits. When a bird is purchased as a result of an informed decision, it is an exception to the rule. Frequently, however, the buyer has some vague awareness of the price ranges for various kinds of birds that may have caught his fancy. If he sees, for example, that Blue Fronted Amazons normally sell at prices ranging from $200-$225, and then notices that advertisements are offering them for sale at bargain-basement prices, he will probably jump at the opportunity to buy what appears to be an exceptional value.

If he buys one of these bargain basement birds, those which were dumped on an 'as is' basis, and the bird is healthy and all that is lacking is time for the bird to grow a new wardrobe of plumage . . . that's good. If he buys a sick bird, however, or a bird which is emaciated from previous diseases, or one whose health has been critically wasted by previous sickness . . . that's bad. At the onset, the bargain basement bird may appear to be a good bargain, but the chances are that the buyer will experience far more grief and problems than he anticipated, sometimes so thoroughly souring him that he may never again purchase another bird, thereby depriving himself of the many pleasures that result through bird ownership.

Again, that is not to suggest that all birds offered at bargain basement prices are birds which should be suspected of being sold by unethical selling practices. Indeed, some sellers may offer particular birds for sale below prevailing prices in order to develop good public relations and a steady clientele. Astute businessmen realize that even should they retail special livestock at or near their cost from time to time, they will still realize a handsome profit because the purchase generally includes the added sale of a cage, various seeds, and diverse paraphernalia needed in the upkeep of the bird.

Diligent shopping can always result in a fine bird at a better price than usual! *But such bird shopping requires an informed consumer.*

A couple of illustrations may be helpful.

The Spectacled Amazon *(Amazona albifrons nana)* is unfortunately not given its just due. A small parrot only ten or so inches long, it is easily tamed and can prove to be a personable bird. Some will even talk. Unfortunately, they are not highly considered because they lack a colorful or outstanding plumage; this, however, does make them very common and inexpensive.

Opposite:
When Richard Favorite first got Rocky, this Green Winged Macaw *(Ara chloroptera)* was a somewhat scraggly looking bird. His disposition, however, is impeccable. He loves to be held by people and is quite content to sit on his master's arm for hours on end if permitted.

This writer once purchased a Double Yellow Head parrot with a deformed beak from a local dealer. Actually, a one-quarter by one-eighth inch chunk of bone had been chipped out of its upper mandible, leaving a gaping hole whenever the beak was shut. When I first noticed that Yellow Head mixed with a group of ten or twelve of his fellows, it soon became apparent what had happened to him. He had taken upon himself to become a self-appointed king of the roost, if you will. He was a virtual despot in that cage, insisting on perching on the food dish. In such a position he could feed himself at will, control the food supply, and ration it to others as he saw fit. Needless to say, the other Yellow Heads did not take too kindly to this absolutism. There was a constant din of bickering and fighting as one or another attempted to dislodge him from his place, apparently without appreciable success. He paid a heavy price, however, in maintaining control of his vantage point, for besides his injured beak, his plumage was somewhat bedraggled with considerable loss of breast plumage. He was a veteran in the real sense of the word.

But it was hard not to take a liking to him for it.

The seller wanted $195 for his Yellows—your choice. I thought it a bit high and said so. Pulling the warrior from the cage, he muttered that he might be able to give me a 'deal' on him. I feigned disinterest, started to walk away, turned around abruptly, and asked how much.

'A hundred and ten dollars,' was the reply. 'Sold,' I said.

Aside from the battle scars, the old despot was in apparent excellent health. Within a few months, he had replaced his shoddy wardrobe with a new set of feathers, and the beak regenerated its missing chunk. He acquired a considerable vocabulary and turned out to be a saucy, affectionate, and charming pet.

In another instance, in complete contrast, an unethical business acquaintance of mine had imported approximately 500 Red Headed Amazons from Mexico. A scant few days before the end of the quarantine period, the flock was stricken by several strains of respiratory diseases which proceeded to ravage the flock. At its worst peak, he was losing as many as 25 birds a day. Different antibiotics were administered to the Red Head, but no sooner did it appear that one epidemic was now under control when another viral strain would sweep through the flock.

58

Since the diseases were domestically originated, release papers were finally issued releasing the Red Heads from quarantine. But so long as the birds were still weak and sickly, this particular importer decided to hold them until they were well on the road to recovery. For the most part they were a sorry lot—thin, emaciated, bedraggled. After they were released, he held them for approximately a week, but because a new shipment of birds was anticipated in the immediate future, this importer had the difficult decision of deciding whether to unload the birds or to house them in another facility, hoping that they would recover quickly and thereby minimizing financial losses. He decided to dispose of the remaining 280 Red Heads at his cost, which was then approximately $20 below the prevailing wholesale price.

At that time, a prime Red Head retailed between $125-$175, depending on the seller. One of the better known livestock handlers in the area bought them 'lock, stock, and barrel,' on an 'as is' basis, for $42 apiece, the prevailing wholesale price being between $60-$65. The birds were then sold at a brisk rate of $79 after a blitzkrieg advertising barrage.

There were several consequences to this bargain basement selling of the Red Heads. In the first place, the $79 price depressed the Red Head market for several weeks afterwards. Moreover, and more importantly, many of the birds purchased from that group died within the next couple of months because of the various complications resulting from their earlier viral infections. Such bargain basement shopping resulted in a lot of broken hearts for both big and little boys and girls.

"Buyer Beware" is always sound advice. A bird recently released from quarantine is not necessarily guaranteed to be in prime health.

Orange Cheeked Amazons *(Amazona autumnalis autumnalis)* are a subspecies of the Red Lored Amazon. Some hobbyists consider the Orange Cheeked Amazon to be an unreliable and unpredictable bird. As in the case of the purchase of any parrot, an Orange Cheeked's disposition should be carefully considered before purchase. They can make good pets and become reasonably good talkers. This fine bird is owned by Ken Fenton of Fountain Valley, California.

Opposite:
The Yellow Naped Amazon is popular among California bird hobbyists. It is an expensive parrot, but because of its unusually good disposition, it is highly prized. This particular bird, called Harriet, is 29 years old. The lovely lady holding the bird is Pat Schneck of Santa Ana, California. Harriet is owned by Dr. K. Svedeen of Mission Viejo, California.

Chapter 4
Buying Baby Parrots

Any discussion of parrots would be remiss if it did not include some consideration of baby parrots. It is an obvious fact that baby parrots, like babies of all mammals and birds, thoroughly endear themselves to all people of all ages. There is something about the infant's helplessness, dependency, and utter trust which never fails to capture even the most insensitive of souls. Who can resist cuddling and protecting a furry, helpless baby?

From a number of perspectives, baby parrots prove to be ideal candidates for pets. Because of their extreme youth, they often become the exception to the rule if they are from a species lacking renown for any one of a variety of traits which may be highly prized by aviculturists. If they are members of a species internationally recognized as being superior to others in a given trait or group of characteristics, they generally prove to be the elite of that species. Succinctly, baby parrots are more apt to talk, to acquire a vocabulary faster, and to develop a more extensive vocabulary than their older fellows. They are also more apt to be amenable, affectionate, and gentle parrots with exceptional personalities.

Most of these kinds of observations are generally already known by the average reader. What is generally not known, however, is that certain kinds of babies are preferable to others. Whenever baby parrots are being offered for sale, they are almost always advertised as 'hand-fed babies.' It is the concept of 'hand-fed babies' which poses a problem and which leads the average bird fancier into failing to draw the distinction between one group of babies being excellent candidates and another group being superior candidates as potential pets.

The problem exists because the term 'hand-fed babies' has always meant in aviculture that a young chick has been *actually* fed by hand since it was a mere few days old. The term as used by many sellers advertising birds with that label *suggests* to the buyer that the bird was fed by hand since birth when in reality it was not.

A seller advertises a particular species of bird as being 'hand-fed.' The bird fancier, knowing that baby birds are better than older birds, visits the seller and finds that indeed this is a baby. It has most of its quill feathers, but its head is still somewhat bald and patches of skin can be seen through its sparse feathers. Usually, too, the baby's breast feathers are matted with a goo which the seller quickly assures the buyer is nothing more than food, for like all other kinds of babies, it gets food all over itself when it eats.

Of course, the baby will be making 'give me some food' demand chirps and an attendant nearby will rush to spoon-feed the bird with a disgusting looking mash which the baby somehow manages to get a bit down its gullet while the rest oozes downward onto its breast feathers.

Certainly there is no question that the bird is a baby chick. It is therefore a 'better' bird than one which may be one, two, or three years old. It also has a better price. A much better price. Actually, the price may be double, triple, or even more than the price of a comparable but older bird of that species, even if that comparable bird is only five months old and no longer has any goo on its breast feathers because it is no longer a baby which cannot feed itself.

There are two questions which demand satisfaction. Is that baby worth a twofold, threefold, or more price because someone is feeding it goo with a spoon? Is that two-month-old chick better than a five- or six-month-old bird, thereby justifying the higher price?

To answer these questions a working definition of 'hand-fed babies' would be helpful. By hand-fed we mean that after hatching the baby chick was taken from its natural mother within a few hours or few days at most and was raised with a human being acting as a surrogate mother. This human being assumed all responsibilities from its natural mother, responsibilities which include feeding the chick and teaching it various types of behaviors.

The responsibility of teaching it various behaviors is a crucial

The cockatiel is easy to breed, and more often than not it is this bird which becomes the starting stock of a novice hobbyist wishing to breed parrots. A 'good' hen will produce five to seven chicks per clutch, two clutches per year. While some breeders have been known to push their hens into three clutches a year, such a policy is self-defeating, for a good hen will soon 'burn' herself out having to care for so many young. The youngster shown here will be fledging within a couple of weeks.

Opposite:
Catalina Macaws are the result of crossing a Scarlet Macaw *(Ara macao)* and a Blue and Gold Macaw *(Ara ararauna).* The top picture shows a Catalina chick being hand-fed, and the bottom photograph shows that the youngster has already learned to perch on its master's arm.

matter. All behavior that a parrot exhibits is the result of two kinds of forces influencing the bird's development. First of all, the bird is born with instinctual patterns built into its system over which it has no control and which therefore predetermine how the bird will act under given sets of circumstances. Hence, for example, it is the bird's instincts which tell the bird when to mate, when to preen itself, when to migrate, how to feed its young, and so on.

Secondly, much of the bird's behavior is learned behavior. That is, during the course of its development after hatching the bird learns from other birds what constitutes appropriate behavior to given sets of conditions. The bird thereby learns from other birds what foods to eat, where to fly to find those foods, what creatures are dangerous to it, what calls to make to indicate danger, and so on.

A young chick reared by a surrogate mother has within its biological system a built-in set of instinctual patterns over which the human has little or no control. But the chick also has built into its biological system an ability to learn, and therefore the content of what the chick learns can be shaped and determined by the surrogate human mother.

The younger the chick when it comes under human influence, the less it has already learned from its natural mother and any other older birds influencing its life. The younger the bird, the greater the tendency to imitate its surrogate mother to the best of its ability. In the biological sciences this process is known as imprinting—that is, the first living thing to come into contact with the young chick during its first few hours of life will be the organism which will have the greatest influence over the future behavioral patterns of the bird.

Obviously then, if we are to train a bird to acquire as many sounds as possible, since most sounds which parrots have are learned sounds, it is best to take the chick from the nest when it is quite young. It is common, therefore, to see such chicks when they are two or three months old already having a vocabulary of several words. An infant chick also learns that the kind of handling it receives from people is natural, and it therefore treats people gently.

For all intents and purposes, a baby reared from birth by a

66

The best pets are those which have been hand-fed while young. This young cockatiel, soon to be independent, will make an exceptional pet. If I were permitted only one choice of all the parrot species as a pet, I would, without question, choose the cockatiel.

The Monk Parakeet *(Myiopsitta monachus)*, sometimes called the Quaker Parakeet, is at times found in aviaries, but it does not prove to be an overall popular species. While it breeds reasonably well in captivity, it lacks popularity because of its lack of marked color and its rejection of humans. The above youngster, 24 days old, is as regrettably unattractive as most infant birds, but despite this unattractiveness, it is still unexplainably 'cute.'

Opposite:
Monk Parakeets are very common in their native South America, and they are one of the few members of the parrot family which build a large nest. This is an adult bird.

human surrogate mother perceives itself as human and tries its best to act like one.

An interesting example of this kind of rearing was, of all things, a duckling raised by my father. Having been born and reared on a farm, my Mom never lost her habit of doing her vegetable and fruit shopping every Saturday at the farmer's market. Each Easter the farmers invariably sold day-old chickens and ducklings. Mom, being what she is, could never resist a baby duckling and one Saturday brought one home. It was my father who had to raise the tiny tike who was subsequently named Nelly.

Now everyone knows that your everyday common old duck is a rather stupid beast. All they really do is go 'quack, quack,' eat, and make a fine Sunday supper. But Mom had to have it because it was cute, downy, and cuddly. Yet being as stupid as ducks may be, Nelly grew up believing she was a human being.

When my parents would sit on the back porch, Nelly would have to sit by their feet. Dad eventually made a small stool for her on which she would sit like everyone else on the porch. If my father went to the garage to putter around, as he usually did, Nelly would also go. When he would cut his front yard, a magnificent carpet to which he devoted great care and time, Nelly invariably would follow in his footsteps as he mowed the lawn or trimmed its edges. If Dad went for a walk to the local tavern for an after-supper glass of beer, Nelly would also go. She even drank beer out of an ashtray that Dad would fill for her.

Nelly also learned the extent of what constituted my father's property. She would never put one webbed foot onto a neighbor's yard. Of course, she never allowed anyone to step foot on Dad's property either. So long as people remained on the city sidewalk they were safe. But should a stranger put a foot on our property, Nelly was prepared to fight.

Once a local television station, hearing of a good human interest story, came to my parents' home to gather some film. They filmed the duck following my father to the tavern. They wanted to film Nelly following my father on his mowing chores. Attempting to film while standing on Dad's lawn, the cameraman was repeatedly chased off onto the public sidewalk. He eventually settled on filming from the sidewalk's safety.

Ducks are stupid and Nelly no less. But Nelly makes a fine

example of an animal with limited ability and intelligence behaving as a result of the imprinting process.

Anyway, an actual hand-fed baby reared by a human being has had a great deal of effort and time invested in the bird. It is a bird so acclimatized to humans and their sounds that it is not infrequent for a breeder to guarantee that the bird will talk. It almost always does already. The higher prices for such birds are therefore not out of line given the quality of the product.

A bird advertised as 'hand fed' when in fact it has not been reared by a human mother is an entirely different story, however. The kind of young chick described in the scenario earlier depicted in this chapter is a bird which was taken from its nest at an age when it was almost totally independent from its mother. By then such a baby parrot has already learned a great deal from its natural mother and has already acquired many distinctive parrot sounds learned from others. It is a bird which, while offering more potential than a one-year-old bird, is not the prime specimen as suggested in 'hand-fed.' In an excellent text on parrots, *Parrots and Related Birds*, (TFH), written by Henry J. Bates and Robert L. Busenbark, edited by Dr. M. M. Vriends, there is a table providing rates of development and growth for various types of parrots which would do much to put the total problem in perspective.

COMPARATIVE NESTING AND REARING PERIODS

Budgerigar: Incubation Period: 18 days; Fledging Age: 5 weeks; Weaning Period: 1 week; Age at Independence: 6 weeks.

Cockatiel: Incubation Period: 18-21 days; Fledging Age: 5 weeks; Weaning Period: 2 weeks; Age at Independence: 7 weeks.

Lovebirds: Incubation Period: 22-25 days; Fledging Age: 6-7 weeks; Weaning Period 2 weeks; Age at Independence: 8-9 weeks.

Parakeets (Elegants and close relatives): Incubation Period: 18 days; Fledging Age: 5 weeks; Weaning Period: 2 weeks; Age at Independence: 7 weeks.

Parakeets (Ringneck family): Incubation Period: 18 days; Fledging Age: 5 weeks; Weaning Period: 4-5 weeks; Age at Independence: 9-10 weeks.

While this young Blue Crowned Lory *(Vini australis)* is somehow hopelessly cute despite its gross unattractiveness, as an adult it will prove to be an attractive bird which is basically green all over. The Blue Crowned is rarely encountered in captivity, and on the rare instance that it is, it invariably is in a zoo.

Opposite:
Adult Blue Crowned Lories are only about seven inches long.

Parrots (Amazons, caiques, African Greys, etc.): Incubation Period: 28 days; Fledging Age: 8 weeks (longer for African Greys); Weaning Period: 5-6 weeks; Age at Independence: 13-14 weeks.

Lories and Lorikeets: Incubation Period: 28 days; Fledging Age: 4-5 weeks; Weaning Period: 4 weeks; Age at Independence: 8-9 weeks.

Cockatoos: Incubation Period: 28 days; Fledging Age: 8 weeks; Weaning Period: 5-6 weeks; Age at Independence: 13-14 weeks.

Macaws: Incubation Period: 28 days; Fledging Age: 12-13 weeks; Weaning Period: 8-10 weeks; Age at Independence: 20-23 weeks.

During the period of development prior to *fledging age,* the young chick is totally dependent on its parent(s) for all protection, food and warmth, and it is still without the primary feathers essential for flight. By *weaning,* it is meant that the parent(s) is teaching the chick to become self-reliant in chewing its own foods and in gathering them. By *age of independence* it is meant that the young adult leaves its parents' care, and while it may still congregate with them in a family or social group, it will no longer be dependent on them for subsistence and protection.

A bird which is a fledgling, therefore, is a helpless chick; a weaning bird is still reliant on its parents but exerting some independence; and a bird at independence no longer needs its parents. Hence, for example, an Amazon parrot is totally dependent on his parents for eight weeks but only needs another five or six weeks to gain full independence. A baby macaw is totally helpless for twelve to thirteen weeks but rapidly learns to become totally self-sufficient within the next 8-10 weeks.

It is obvious that during the weaning period many species of young birds are already becoming independent. Many young birds being weaned are already capable of flight, have often already left their nest, and for the most part can take relatively good care of themselves.

Most of the so-called 'hand-fed babies' being offered for sale are indeed being hand-fed, but they are also young birds which are at the stage of weaning and, depending on their species, can take some care of themselves. *They are young chicks which were taken from their nests just as the weaning period was beginning, or just slightly before.* They are birds, therefore, who have learned most of the rudimentary skills needed for survival from their natural parents. Some of them are so close to total independence that they can begin cracking their own seeds, but their sellers can extend the length of weaning by continuing to spoon-feed them instead of introducing them to seeds and other foods. This writer once saw a fully feathered Red Headed Amazon being spoon-fed and treated as a baby. The price tag was $399 while comparably aged Red Heads from competitive sellers were selling for $150-$200.

In short, while a young parrot of weaning age is obviously a bird with better potential than a much older bird, it is by no means such a prize that its potential buyer should pay no attention to other factors.

These kinds of birds are still capable of learning many things, for they are still young and relatively flexible. They also endure stress much better than adult birds. They are not, however, worth the over-inflated prices asked for them. While the price difference between such a bird and a five- to six-month older brother is substantial, the difference in their learning potential is minimal.

Baby birds make excellent candidates for pets. If a weaning baby raised by natural parents is being sold as a hand-fed baby, *but its price is not out of line with slightly older birds of the same species,* buy it. For a week or so additional effort may be needed in the caring of the bird until it becomes totally independent, but the rewards may very well be worth the greater effort required.

Should a truly hand-fed baby bird be the heart's desire, then the buyer must be prepared to pay a substantial difference over what would be normally expected. The labor costs in rearing the young chick are extensive because it must be constantly fed, particularly during its first few days of life. Moreover, many species of parrots breed very poorly while in captivity so that with some of the more exotic species, when there is a successful nesting, the happy event makes the headlines in aviculture magazines. Some species breed so rarely in captivity that often there are considerably long waiting lists of aviculturists eager to get a hand-fed baby. In short, there are many bird fanciers willing to pay premium prices for the hand-fed young of exotic and rarer species, particularly when they are noted for characteristics which make them excellent pets.

While Senegal Parrots *(Poicephalus senegalus)* are common household pets in Europe, they are somewhat rare in North America. This parrot has a reputation for being a delightful, docile pet, but some individuals are ornery. These hand-fed babies will prove to be charming.

Opposite:
When buying a Senegal, one should be sure that the parrot is already tame or, preferably, that it is a youngster whose eyes are still black rather than yellow, the adult coloration. Wild adult Senegals often do not respond favorably to taming.

The best source for a truly hand-fed baby is, of course, a legitimate breeder with an established breeding program for various species of parrots. Such breeders are always proud of their successful breeding programs and are therefore flattered when asked for a tour of the premises. The prospective buyer will have a first-hand opportunity to see for himself nesting hens, attendants feeding chicks, and so on.

In the colder regions of the country where breeding programs are more difficult to establish, a prospective buyer can order a hand-fed chick from any one of a variety of breeders in other regions of the country. Breeders' advertisements are common in avicultural publications which may be found in any public library. The buyer need not worry about ordering a prized bird in this manner. Most breeders guarantee live delivery, and many private ones will provide affidavits testifying to the young bird being hand-fed since infancy.

When buying a hand-fed bird from other sellers, however, considerable caution should be exercised. Many so-called hand-fed birds can already say a word or two, and the uninitiated can often be very easily deceived. The novice bird buyer is thus at a tremendous disadvantage, for, unless the seller is prepared to supply the buyer with the name and address of the breeder, there is really no way of knowing whether the bird was truly hand-fed since birth and therefore raised by a human surrogate mother. This would not be a problem if it was not for the fact that many prized species are extremely expensive to begin with and hand-fed babies even more expensive.

Without definite proof of the bird having been surrogate-mothered, it is best to forget about the bird and buy one instead which is a few months older and considerably cheaper or buy a legitimately hand-fed baby from a breeder.

Don't let your feelings of tenderness for the tyke and the goo on his breast feathers carry you away so that you dig deep into your pocket.

A final word about babies and young parrots. If we again look at the nesting-and-rearing table printed earlier, we will note, for example, that macaws become independent at between 20 and 23 weeks of age. Most macaws do not reach full maturity until they are five to seven years old. A macaw, therefore, if we can apply human terms to it, is an adolescent at three or four years of age. It is *still* a young bird and, while it may have established its own sets of behavior and therefore be more difficult to tame, train, and to teach to talk, it is still amenable to human influences. Of course, a three-year-old macaw is less desirable than a one-year-old macaw, but that does not mean that the macaw is not going to make a good pet. The same is true of other parrots and parrot types.

Unless one is prepared to pay premium prices for actual hand-fed babies, it is best to locate a young bird which is still, relatively speaking, an adolescent. There are numerous parrot books on the market which provide color, size and other differentials distinguishing mature from immature parrots. Failing a book, any reputable pet shop proprietor will be glad to locate an immature bird which will retail at the prevailing prices at that time for its species.

Red Headed Amazons *(Amazona viridigenalis)* are popular and inexpensive pets. While it is only a minority which do talk, they do make good pets. Red Heads can be somewhat chattery, however. This youngster, held by Chris Espinoza of Norwalk, California, was handfed. The bird is owned by Richard Favorite of Norwalk, California.

Opposite:
This beautiful creature is a hybrid between a Green Winged Macaw *(Ara chloroptera)* and a Scarlet Macaw *(Ara macao).* Happy was born at Lion Country Safari in Laguna Hills, California. She was bought by her present owners when she was still unfeathered and being hand-fed. She is owned by Bob Branch of Garden Grove, California.

Chapter 5
Symptoms of Bad Health

Just as with human beings, there are no guarantees concerning health and life for birds. All mortal beings become sick and must eventually die, some sooner than others. It would be unreasonable to expect a pet dealer to guarantee that any exotic bird he sells will live a healthy life leading to longevity. But one can expect, and indeed should even demand, that a bird be healthy and free of serious disorders at the time of purchase.

It is unfortunately true that many exotic birds retailed by livestock dealers are sick at the time of sale, some of them mortally ill—so ill that they do not survive the first two or three weeks of new ownership. Much of this health problem can be frankly attributed to the unethical business practices of a minority of livestock dealers who know and even sometimes deliberately retail exotic birds whose health is failing and whose death is highly imminent within a short time of purchase. Such merchants prey on the general lack of knowledge that a customer brings with him into the store. By selling such birds, unscrupulous sellers can effectively minimize their unrecoverable losses.

Some of the problem, too, can be attributed to sellers whose general knowledge of bird health is so limited that they lack even the most rudimentary diagnostic skills needed in order to maintain their stock in a healthy condition. These people are of course deplored by everyone in the bird field—but they will continue to exist as long as potential purchasers seek "bargains." Sometimes, too, a bird suffering from an illness is sold when there is no obvious indication to even the best of discerning eyes of customers and dealer alike that the bird is ill. Sadly, it is almost always the customer who bears the full brunt of the loss should the bird die.

There is little a bird fancier can do to protect himself should he purchase an expensive exotic bird that seems to enjoy excellent health when in fact the ravages of an illness are already beginning to manifest themselves in the bird's system. These things happen, just as with people who might have their annual medical check-up today only to die of a heart attack a few days later after being declared hale and hearty.

But a prospective buyer can guard himself by arming himself with rudimentary skills that will help him to recognize the various characteristics which might identify sickness in a bird. And, in defense of the pet industry, many dealers do offer contracts guaranteeing that their birds are free from *immediate* sickness. That is, they guarantee that the bird is healthy when purchased and that for a specified period of time, should the bird die, some compensation will be awarded the purchaser. Sometimes, if the guarantee is for a longer period than a week or two, the guarantee may be contingent on the results of an autopsy to determine the cause of death. Since some diseases require lengthy incubation periods, the bird may have already been ill at the time of purchase, thereby providing the customer with a measure of protection. But an autopsy also reveals whether the bird died as a result of abuse or stress or from inadequate care while in the custody of the owner.

The United States Department of Agriculture performs autopsies at the cost of only a few dollars. It is always wise to have a dead bird autopsied if there are other birds in the household or if a new bird is to be purchased in order to replace the dead pet. Should the death have resulted from a highly contagious disease, future loss can be prevented by sterilizing the premises and taking various other steps to ensure the continued health of present and future birds in the home.

Regardless of whether a pet dealer offers a guarantee or not, however, a prospective buyer should always astutely examine a bird before making the final decision. A careful and thorough examination—indeed, even a medical check-up by a competent veterinarian specializing in avian diseases—may not necessarily ensure the customer that the bird will not become mortally ill in the near future after purchase, but such an examination will go a long way towards reducing the possibility of buying a sick bird. Once the bird has left the store, guarantee or no guarantee, a sick bird invariably becomes the problem of the owner.

This Scarlet Macaw, Gypsy, is at least fifty years old. She was previously owned by a lady for forty years, during which time the bird had nothing to do but sit between two food cups on a perch. Out of sheer boredom she began plucking her feathers as they grew in, a habit she still carries on with her new owner, Bob Branch of Garden Grove, California. All parrots should be given toys to chew; such activities are needed to maintain good emotional health.

Of the three subspecies of the African Grey Parrot, the Red Tailed African Grey *(Psittacus erithacus erithacus)* is the most popular and the best in disposition. Greys are almost always easily trained, although even when tamed they will growl a great deal. The young adult held by Bob Goehle was just recently released from a holding station and is already a gentle pet. The bird is owned by Dr. K. Svedeen.

Exotic birds suffer from a wide variety of sicknesses and ailments. The purpose and scope of this book is so limited that it would be impossible to instruct the layman in so brief a time in the essential characteristics of every health problem affecting birds so that the reader would become a diagnostician and expert on avian diseases. Several years of intensive study are required before a veterinarian can develop and master such skills.

Instead, our purpose is to provide the reader with sufficient basic concepts so that he will be better able to recognize a sick bird. By knowing what to look for, he will be a better judge in choosing a healthy bird instead of a sick one and will be in a better position to recognize when his pet requires professional treatment

In discussing the general symptoms indicative of poor health, there is always the risk that the reader who is becoming an amateur aviculturist will invariably make the wrong decisions for the wrong reasons. To use a pair of hackneyed cliches, it is often said that a little knowledge can be a dangerous thing, for some people are quick to make mountains out of molehills. Because a bird may display any one of the symptoms that will be discussed shortly, that does not necessarily mean that the bird will drop dead the next moment. Perhaps the bird, like you and me, just doesn't feel well, and for no special reason. Indigestion. A chill perhaps.

However, should the prospective pet capturing the eye of the buyer display any one of the kinds of symptoms we will be concerned with, the purchase should not be made in haste, regardless of how appealing the bird may be. And if one's pet displays symptoms of sickness the master should keep careful watch so as to determine whether the symptoms are indicative of some minor discomfort or a more serious disorder.

For a working definition, good health can be defined as the disposition to display behavior which is usual to the species, which is alert and cheerful, and in which the bodily functions are performing normally as needed to maintain the homeostasis required for the continuation of its normal, usual behavior. A sick bird is an organism which is prevented from performing its normal functions because of some disruption in its biological equilibrium so that there is obvious deviation from its usual day-to-day behavior.

The effects of these disruptions can often be observed in any one of a variety of possible symptoms; some of them are obvious while others are more subtle. Sometimes, given a symptom, there is no way of knowing whether the bird is suffering from a minor malaise or a more serious disorder, whereas other symptoms clearly define the seriousness of the problem. Sometimes, several symptoms occur concurrently, particularly when the illness has progressed into an acute stage of development. At other times, there may be an absence of obvious symptoms until the terminal stages of the disease when death is imminent. At times, a bird may display one symptom or another which may indicate only a minor problem, but the appearance of the same symptoms on other occasions may indicate the cumulative development of a more critical problem. In short, just as with humans, there is no over-all distinct pattern, because there are many sicknesses that may affect the bird in various degrees of seriousness.

Finally, for those readers who already own exotic birds, it would be wise to keep a close watch over the bird should its behavior be symptomatic of some type of ailment. When sick, birds, like all other animal life, generally lose their appetite and stop eating properly. As their intake of nutrition decreases, not only does their current health problem worsen, but their susceptibility to various other more serious diseases increases. A simple cold, for example, which is not necessarily a killer, will reduce the bird's ability to thwart the development of a later, more serious sickness because resistance has been severely diminished as a result of reduced nutritional intake. It has been observed that sick birds who refuse to eat for four or five days can lose up to a third of their body weight!

There are some diseases, however, in which the bird eats heartily until a short time before death. In such cases, nevertheless, the eating behavior itself may become a clue as to the bird's deteriorating health condition. For example, it may be drinking massive quantities of water, far more than usual; it may eat only soft foods, rejecting even the hard ones which were previously favorites; and so on.

Should symptoms persist after a couple of days, therefore, the wisest course of action is to immediately seek professional veterinary help before the weight loss can become a major problem.

This trio of characters is the delight of Ken and Linda Fenton of Fountain Valley, California. They are named Baby (Lesser Sulphur Crested Cockatoo), Babe (Moluccan Cockatoo) and Bamby (Medium Sulphur Cockatoo). As soon as their cages are uncovered in the morning, the two Sulphurs immediately join Babe on his perch. They are content to sit for hours on end together with most of the time spent in mutual preening and cuddling. They are an absolute delight to hold and to behold.

Regardless of what they do, where they are or what mischief they are involved in planning, this trio always shows an interest in what is taking place. Usually, while the Moluccan remains calm and composed all of the time, the two Sulphurs will always raise their crests when things just don't look right to them. I tried to get them to raise their crests—all to no avail. The only reactions I seemed to get were 'Who is this nutty photographer?' by the Sulphurs and a 'Who really cares?' reaction from the Moluccan.

GENERAL HEALTH AND
OVERALL APPEARANCE

A healthy bird is an organism which shows vitality in its appearance and behavior. It is cheerful and animated even during its quieter moments when it may be resting. While it may snooze or rest now and then during the day, particularly if it is a young bird, such activities do not occupy a great deal of a bird's daylight hours. It is a bird which flaps its wings, hops about its cage, climbs the bars, cleans its feet, rubs its beak against a cuttlebone or perch, begs for tidbits, bites people if it is still wild, seeks attention if it's spoiled, squawks loudly for no apparent reason, quarrels with its neighbors, sings, mutters to itself, scolds people, whistles, preens itself, chews its perch, and does any one of a multitude of other activities which are common to its species.

It is a bird which never fails to astound its master with its enormous appetite. Indeed, it seems to devour vast quantities of seeds, fresh fruits and greens, seeming to be forever eating, and the wonder never ceases how such a 'little bird' can put away 'so much food.' The truth is that a bird's metabolism is so designed that all food is processed within a very few short hours, thereby necessitating further eating behavior if the bird is to keep from being hungry. In this manner some species of birds actually consume up to a third of their body weight per day. Indeed, as already noted earlier, a decreased appetite is always symptomatic of some type of serious disorder affecting the bird.

Healthy birds exhibit all these kinds of activities and more. There is a glow and sheen to their plumage and a vitality which is sharply contrasted when compared with an ill bird. The bird's behavior and its general appearance are therefore always some indication as to the state of the bird's health.

Too often, unfortunately, the condition of a bird's plumage is frequently the criterion that many novice bird enthusiasts use in deciding whether or not to buy a specific bird. Because a bird's plumage may be somewhat dilapidated when compared to the plumage of the specimen models photographed for parrot books, that does not necessarily mean that the bird is ill. The bird may have just been released from a quarantine station where the cage conditions are so poor that opportunities for appropriate self-grooming are virtually non-existent. Or, the bird may be molting and its feathers have yet to be replaced. These are certainly legitimate appearance problems which are no cause for alarm should the bird be healthy in all other ways.

But a dilapidated appearance may also be indicative of poor health in general. A bird's feathers are a reflection of both its emotional state and the bird's bodily processes. A physically healthy bird produces plumage with a sheen common to its species. As feathers are lost for one reason or another, nature replaces them to match them exactly in color and appearance. A sick bird, however, lacks the internal resources and body tonality necessary in growing and maintaining a healthy feathered appearance.

Similarly, a bird's emotional state is directly related to its appearance. A healthy bird is forever grooming itself as if romance was just around the corner. It pulls its feathers through its beak to clean and rearrange them. Some species have glands which secrete oils or powders which the bird uses to add luster and protection to its feathers. An emotionally and physically healthy bird is a bird concerned about its appearance.

Even when the bird's feathers seem an impossible dream to restore, a healthy bird will continue to preen itself as best it can, pulling at tattered and dirty feathers over and over again in its vanity. On the other hand, an exotic bird which seems to be the epitome of health and vitality because of a wardrobe of magnificent plumage may in fact be ill if it is not concerned with maintaining its appearance.

When buying an exotic bird, therefore, its general appearance, grooming behavior, and various assorted bird activities are excellent reflections of the bird's physical and emotional states and whether or not the bird is ill.

Plumpness

Birds which are ill or have just undergone an illness are birds which have generally suffered a significant weight loss. An attractive wardrobe of feathers, unfortunately, easily conceals the wasted and ravaged condition of the bird's body. It is therefore always prudent to examine the bird's degree of plumpness.

A plump bird is a bird which has not only been well-fed, but it is an animal which has not recently suffered a disease which has wasted its fat resources. The kind of plumpness referred to here is

Umbrella Cockatoos *(Cacatua alba)*, often called White Cockatoos, are native to eastern Indonesia. They prove to be gentle creatures with a dignified demeanor. This fellow, tamed by me, was named Clem because he would balk at doing any sort of work, but he would never bite. Clem is owned by Richard Favorite.

The Blue Fronted Amazon *(Amazona aestiva aestiva)* is a parrot whose habitat stretches from northeastern Brazil to central Argentina. This parrot has a good disposition and, unlike many other Amazon parrots, is more predictable in behavior; it is a rare Blue Fronted which is mean or untamable. Because of its ability to mimic, it is a contender for a position in the top five best talkers. This fellow overheard a group of youngsters playing cowboys and Indians, and a couple of days later I was surprised to hear the neigh of a horse immediately followed by the pow-pow-pow of an imaginary pistol being fired.

93

the kind that Grandmother searched for at the weekly farmer's market when she would shop for a live chicken for Sunday dinner. She would probe the bird's breast, and if the breast bone was sticking out, she would reject it as a skinny and unpalatable chicken. The kind of plumpness she looked for is the kind we are concerned with; namely, fatness is an excellent sign of good health.

If the breast is plump, the kind one would expect in order to have a succulent chicken dinner, or parrot dinner for that matter, then the parrot is a good candidate for a pet, regardless of how ragged the feathers may appear. That is assuming that there are no other symptoms indicating a deterioration of health.

But if the breast bone is sticking out, then it is best to forget about that particular parrot, irrespective of how attractive and animated it may be. The bird has either just recovered from a disease or is beginning to experience the later stage of disease development at which point it may still outwardly appear to be enjoying good health. Its reduced and emaciated condition reveals a concurrent reduction in internal resources required to combat sickness.

Even if the bird is on a rapid recovery from an earlier sickness, it is still best to avoid the purchase of such livestock. Because it was

A well-muscled breast is a sign of a healthy bird. Feel the breast when choosing your parrot, and check it periodically to be sure it's staying in good health.

ill, its diminished resistance and resources make it susceptible to other possible infections and diseases. If at all in doubt, don't buy the bird. There are other specimens of the same species which can be found in any number of other exotic bird outlets.

This writer has seen some sick birds passed off as healthy animals which were so emaciated that the forefinger and thumb could actually grab a full quarter of an inch of breast bone which was virtually free of flesh except for skin. These unfortunate creatures were nothing more than a shadow of life on the verge of death.

The reader should not feel self conscious about asking the pet dealer to permit an inspection of plumpness. A conscientious livestock dealer proud of the fine health of his livestock will be only too pleased to prove to his customers that his birds are indeed prime and healthy. If the bird is tame, so much the better; have it sit on the arm and gently run the forefinger and thumb over the breast bone. If the bird is still wild and difficult to manage, have the dealer hold the bird in a constrained manner so that the plumpness can be examined. Besides, by having him hold the bird, there is less risk in getting bitten oneself.

Neurotic Parrots

Most wild parrots clearing a quarantine station are birds which for all intents and purposes do not differ significantly in behavior from when they were still free in the wilds. They still have the same instinctual patterns of behavior as previously, and should they be released to their wild haunts, they would not differ much from their previous patterns of behavior.

Some of these parrots can be said to differ, however, in a positive way. Their capture, captivity, and contact with men has resulted in the parrot acquiring various patterns of behavior which make it more tame than its caged brothers. Captivity and contact with men have taught the parrot new patterns of behavior by which it relates differently to men than those which have not changed. Such parrots, even during the quarantine period itself, seem to be less afraid than their fellows; they may even accept tidbits of food offered by the keeper. These kinds of parrots are 'cherries' in the sense that it is immediately recognized that they are

Finsch's Amazons *(Amazona finschi)* are one of the more common Amazon parrots found in the United States. Native to Mexico, there are two subspecies of this fine bird. Sometimes called the Lilac Crowned Amazon, they make good pets even though there are not too many that talk. When they are kept in good health and given ample opportunity to take care of their plumage, it will have an iridescent quality which is not frequently found in other Amazons. This lovely bird is owned by Lindsay Salathiel of Newport Beach, California.

Opposite:
Parrotlets are small South American birds which resemble lovebirds. Parrotlets have been bred in captivity, but they are generally not very popular because they lack outstanding color and they are not very easy to tame. Shown is a Green-Rumped Parrotlet *(Forpus passerinus)*.

fast learners and will make ideal pets. (Usually, these exceptional birds are already picked out and claimed before the birds have even cleared the required quarantining period.)

There are other exceptional birds, however, which have learned to react to captivity and men in a totally negative pattern of behavior. Because of the handling they have received, and the manner in which they have been handled, these parrots have learned to respond to captivity and men in ways which make them undesirable as pets because it will be difficult, if not impossible, to change their responses into the kinds of constructive behaviors needed if a creature is to become a pet. While some may argue that there is no such thing as a neurotic parrot, the fact is that there are birds which depart from the behavior expected under normal conditions.

We can describe neurotic behavior as those responses which are abnormal under certain conditions and which are detrimental to the parrot's health and to its relationships with men. An example may be helpful in putting our definition into perspective.

Let us assume that we have a hundred Triton Cockatoos in quarantine and it is now their fourth week in confinement. Most of the Tritons will behave similarly. Most will be afraid when the attendants approach the cages to clean them and feed the birds. Some will cower, some will cry out in fright, some will scramble from cage-side to cage-side until the threat has passed. This is normal behavior because they are still wild and act accordingly.

There will be a few, however, which will remain relatively unmoved by the fact that a hand has entered the cage, has removed and replaced food and water dishes, and perhaps has even attempted to touch the bird. These exceptional birds have soon learned that there is little to fear from men. These are the 'cherries' that we mentioned earlier.

There will be a few others, however, which will be neither normal nor 'cherry' in behavior. Instead of just cowering or crying out in fear, these birds shriek in terror. When the attendant has approached the cage, he may have noticed that the parrot remained fixed in one space, perhaps with its bill hooked firmly on a cage wire. The Triton may remain like that for hours. While the others are reacting in their usual wild fashion, this bird's behavior stands out just as does a 'cherry's' behavior.

Some time ago I received a telephone call from a man who had purchased a Severe Macaw, who had worked with it, and who was totally unable to make any progress in taming it. He brought the bird over. It seemed a young macaw, perhaps only two years old.

In the four days which I had the bird, it never moved once from the right hand side of the cage. It was fixed there. One foot on its food dish, the other foot on the perch, its beak locked on a cage bar. When I tried to remove the parrot from the cage, it retained its position but would screech through its semi-closed beak. After nine twenty minute sessions trying to work with the bird, I had made absolutely no progress to speak of. The bird was wild, but the fact is it was also neurotic, a fact I was aware of after the second day but which I nevertheless ignored because of the challenge this particular bird presented.

There is no way of fully guaranteeing that a bird is not neurotic. But, when shopping for parrots, it is wise to pay attention and to become accustomed to normal parrots in both wild and tame states of the species one is interested in. All wild parrots will react similarly. All tamed parrots of a species will react similarly. When a parrot departs in behavior from that similarity with others in the same state of tameness, it is best to observe that parrot over a period of time before making the decision to buy it.

While a physically ill bird can be cured and can become a healthy specimen when given the proper drugs, a neurotic bird is difficult to cure. The neurotic patterns of behavior must be unlearned and the processes totally reversed. This is an extremely difficult task when it comes to animals. One need only consider how difficult it is to cure a human being of a neurotic tendency, such as an abnormal fear of heights or snakes, and it becomes immediately obvious that the task is fundamentally an impossible one when it comes to animals.

Weakness Characteristics

As mentioned earlier, a healthy bird is forever 'doing his thing.' Between climbing about its cage, squawking, feeding, and preening itself, it is sitting on its perch and doing whatever birds like to do when they are just sitting there. Healthy birds respond to both their internal and external environments. They are active and cheerful. If wild, they will bite you if feeling threatened; and if

The Malabar Parakeet *(Psittacula columboides)*, sometimes called the Blue Winged Parakeet, is a native of southwestern India. It is one of the most beautiful of all the parakeet group, but it is rarely encountered in captivity. It is highly prized by aviculturists.

Opposite:
The Moustached Parakeet *(Psittacula alexandri fasciata)* is a popular bird in aviaries, particularly because of its beautiful plumage. This lovely parrot is generally about fifteen inches in length. This specimen is owned by Busch Bird Sanctuary in Van Nuys, California.

they are tame they will incessantly expect you to scratch their heads.

A bird which is ill, however, is a bird which lacks spontaneity and alertness. Depending on the severity and duration of its sickness, it will be experiencing some degree of weakness. The more extreme the ravages affecting its health, the greater its discomfort and weakness and the less alert and spontaneous its behavior. A sickened bird does not hop about its cage in its usual pursuit of everyday business. It sits on its perch hours on end, sleeping a great deal for movement rapidly brings on exhaustion; often there is virtually no movement whatever. If the bird is in a terminal stage of a sickness, and close to death, it may even be forced to abandon its perch because it is too weak to continue grasping the perch and maintain its balance. On the floor, it will support itself with its tail, sitting there just as motionless as before. When death is imminent, the bird might even be unable to hold its head up.

If the bird is still wild, it can often be picked up with a minimum of protest or biting behavior: the bird has become so weak that it shows virtually no recognition of danger or interest in defending itself. If the bird is tame, it will make no effort to solicit head scratchings and it will reject most offerings of its most favorite foods. Should it accept a tidbit, it may drop it because it may be too weak to feed itself. If one should attempt to hand-feed the bird, it may even be too weak to chew and swallow the food.

When the sickness of a bird has progressed to the kinds of weaknesses in the example described above, the bird has lost its ability to respond to its environment regardless of how rewarding or threatening it may be. The prognosis for recovery of such birds is poor.

Usually, a bird enthusiast will rarely encounter a sick bird at this stage of terminality in a pet shop. The dealer will have discreetly written the parrot off as a "croaker" and will have removed it from the cages. Of importance, nevertheless, is the fact that a sick bird is one which shows decreasing interest in internal and external environmental stimuli. As the disease progresses, the bird weakens and attempts to husband its strength and resources.

Birds which appear to lack spontaneity, alertness, cheerfulness, and which appear to be apathetic, whether they are tame or wild, are birds which should be highly suspect ... and avoided.

Bird Droppings

The coloration and consistency of a bird's droppings are strong indications of the condition of a bird's health. Each discharge from the vent consists of both urine and feces, the liquids being the urine and the thicker wastes the feces. A normal healthy bird's droppings are dark grayish to grayish green in color with lighter grayish white strands appearing in the thicker wastes. When the bird drops its wastes while sitting on the perch, the waste forms a clump on the floor of the cage because the consistency of the waste product is relatively thick.

A sick bird's droppings will vary significantly in both color and consistency from a healthy bird's wastes. The droppings may be soft, watery, thin, dry, thick, gummy, or viscid; they may also be almost colorless, clear, bright green, bloody, gray, white, yellow, green, or brown. The colors and the consistency are often enough evidence to suggest the type of ailment which may be affecting the bird.

Sometimes the appearance of the droppings indicates nothing more than some minor digestive disorders brought about by stale foods, lack of sufficient exercise, insufficient minerals in the diet, a switch from normal to new and strange foods, or an insufficient amount of greens or fruits. Frequently, however, the same colorings and consistency may be indicative of serious disorders which could prove to be fatal.

At the risk of appearing tactless, a bird fancier should become acquainted with the appearance of normal bird droppings from a healthy bird. A change in the color and consistency is often one of the first clues indicating sickness. Should a prospective bird be particularly appealing but its droppings deviate from the usual color and consistency, the problem may simply be nothing more than a minor ailment without cause for alarm. But should the droppings appear abnormal and there are other symptoms such as ruffled feathers, the bird is probably ill enough to avoid buying it, irrespective of how appealing the parrot may be otherwise.

Ruffled Feathers

Most birds ruffle their feathers from time to time and frequently maintain them in ruffled states when they are resting, snoozing, or sleeping. At all other times a healthy bird's feathers are normally

103

The Mallee Ringneck Parakeet *(Barnardius barnardi)* is sometimes called Barnard's Parakeet. This attractive Australian bird, while sometimes encountered in the collections of advanced hobbyists, is rarely available.

Opposite:

The Port Lincoln Parakeet *(Barnardius zonarius zonarius),* native to southern Australia, is similar to the Mallee in that it is a lovely colored bird which is not often seen in captivity.

held close to the body, streamlining it for reduced wind resistance in flight. Fluffed up feathers act to better insulate the body, thereby conserving its heat during those times when the body's metabolism slows down as in when the bird is sleeping. Ruffling feathers during time of inactivity is therefore a perfectly normal behavior for a healthy bird.

Ruffled feathers, however, can suggest that the bird is suffering from a fever and that it is attempting to husband its body warmth. Usually, when a bird is sick and there are ruffled feathers, there are also other general symptoms indicating sickness, symptoms such as inactivity, heavy panting, loss of appetite, and so on.

It is extremely easy to mistake ruffled feathers as being symptomatic of some serious illness affecting the bird. The bird may, in fact, just be resting, or perhaps it is experiencing some minor discomfort whose presence is no reason for alarm. But if there are other symptomatic characteristics of sickness present, there is definite reason for concern.

Another indication that a bird is suffering from a sickness or ailment which results in a fever is the manner in which the bird folds its wings to its body. A healthy bird, when sitting on a perch, will hold its wings close to the body, aside from the times that it may stretch or flap them. When a fever is ravaging a bird, the bird often feels too warm and it will therefore open its wings from its body instead of keeping them closely folded as usual. There is a resulting gap between body and wing. With the larger parrots, the gap may be large enough so that a thumb can easily be inserted between wing and body without disturbing the feathers. The smaller birds, of course, gap their wings proportionate to their size.

Whatever the case, when the wings are not held tightly to the body the bird is generally overheated. It may very well be overheated because the bird has worked hard in training, because the bird has been overactive in its play while climbing about in its cage, or because the temperature of the room is becoming unbearably warm. But wing gap may also be evidence of a fever-producing disease.

Wing gap may be maintained by an overheated bird which is overworked, overplayed, or overheated until the bird begins to again feel comfortable, at which time the wings are again appropriately pressed to the body. With a sick bird, however, wing gap may be intermittent throughout the day as the fever ravages the body, alternating between hot, cold, and normal. When the bird is ill and feverish, wing gap will occur when there has been no activity on the part of the bird and no environmental unusualness.

Frequently, concurrent with ruffled feathers and wing gap, the bird will be noticed to have spasms of heavy panting behavior. The panting may be erratic in that the bird may have the panting spasms without any specific pattern to them; a fit of panting behavior lasting a few seconds may be noticed without a reoccurrence happening at any predictable time. There is usually no observable cause for the panting such as would be the case had the parrot been vigorously climbing about the cage. Panting behavior is almost always an indication of feverish conditions.

Breathing Patterns

The manner in which a bird breathes may also be indicative of a wide range of respiratory diseases which may be caused by viral, bacterial, parasitic or fungal agents. Usually, respiratory diseases result in symptoms similar to the kinds of symptoms arising from digestive disorders, circulatory problems, and so on. Droppings may assume an abnormal coloration and consistency, feathers may be ruffled, etc.

In most types of respiratory sicknesses, however, there are also distinct changes from the usual in the bird's breathing behavior. The bird may appear to have considerable difficulty breathing; it may breathe open-mouthed; breathing may be rapid, spasmodic; there may be considerable coughing, sneezing; breathing may sound rasping and asthmatic, and should the bird's breast be placed against the ear, the raspy breathing of the laboring lungs will be heard.

With various diseases, various other symptoms of abnormality reveal themselves. A bird whose species is noted for its song may sing at lower and lower pitches, each succeeding series of notes in lower pitch than before; sometimes the bird may not sing at all. While appearing normal in every other way, the ailing bird may sit puffed up like a furry ball.

In a disease called gape, caused by a parasitic worm infesting lung tissue, the bird will make unusual gaping motions with its

Pesquet's Parrot *(Psittrichas fulgidas)* is a somewhat unattractive parrot which inhabits Papua New Guinea. While it is common in the wild and is available for importation, its drab appearance when compared with other more colorful parrot species probably accounts for its rarity abroad.

Opposite:
The Mealy Amazon *(Amazona farinosa)* comprises five distinct subspecies. The Mealy is a large bird, heavily built, and has a dignified demeanor even when wild. While it is a relatively plain-looking bird, it can be a good talker. This Mealy, owned by Ken Fenton of Fountain Valley, California, is a mild-mannered bird even though he has somehow lost several breast feathers.

head thrusting forward, its beak wide open, and with its neck working as if to dislodge something from its throat. The symptoms are unmistakable.

Finally, plugged nostrils are often a symptom of various respiratory sicknesses. They may be plugged with cheese-like materials to the extent that the pressures within the nasal cavaties may even split the upper part of the upper mandible adjoining the skull. The nostrils may exude watery materials as in the case of a common cold affecting man. While plugged nostrils themselves should not be a matter of over concern, when accompanied by other symptoms, there should be caution exercised before a final decision to purchase the bird is made.

Eye Condition

Eyes which are partially or totally closed are indicative of a number of diseases. While an eye may be closed because of some foreign matter which has entered it and which is thereby irritating the eye tissue, more often than not the eye is closed because of disease. Clear liquids may ooze from the corners of the infected organ. The feathers around the eye and cheek will be wet and matted. When the infection has closed the eye and the lids are forced open, there is often an accumulation of pus underneath. Whether the eye is closed or not, the lids will be observed to be red and inflamed.

Be wary of such birds, even though the salesperson may seem assuring that the problem is nothing more than a simple eye irritation brought about by some foreign substance underneath the lids. While many eye infections can be treated with reasonable success, in a disease called conjunctivitis (which is highly contagious) partial or total blindness may result regardless of treatment. A common disease, conjunctivitis is responsible for blindness in fifty percent of the birds which contract it.

If it appears that a livestock dealer has an epidemic of eye infections and that a prospective bird of your interest has been treated for it, check the eye for blindness. An easy way, of course, is to move the hand or object past the suspected eye, and if there is no corresponding head movement, the bird may be blind on that side. Sometimes, when the bird has been blinded in an eye, there will be a white spot like a pinhead of white lint in the vicinity of the pupil.

Broken Wings

Given that birds are as fragile as they are, it is truly remarkable that more birds do not receive broken wings than they do as a result of the rough treatment they receive during handling when they are wild. Yet broken wings, while they do occur on occasion, are not such a frequent problem as are the more common diseases and ailments which plague exotic birds.

A broken wing can easily be identified because the wing, when folded against the body, droops very obviously so that, depending on the broken bone, the tip may even actually touch the perch. When treated and set by a veterinarian, a broken wing mends easily and quickly. However, a seller who knowingly sells an exotic bird with a broken limb should be avoided for obvious reasons.

Sanitary Conditions in Pet Shops

It is an axiom that cleanliness is akin to godliness. Any person earning his livelihood from the sale of livestock has an obligation to both his stock and customers in maintaining his livestock in good health and in the prevention of disease. An ethical and conscientious dealer will insist on sanitary conditions in his store at all times.

Cages will be cleaned daily. Water will be changed daily. The birds will daily be given an ample supply of fresh fruits, greens, and seeds, as appropriate to each species; the previous day's leftovers will be thrown out. The avian room will be sunny if possible, and if not, brightly lit with artificial lights.

The walls and floors will be free of roaches, insects, and various other vermin. Sick birds will be separated and quarantined from the healthy birds. Birds will have ample room in their cage permitting them to conduct their normal activities without undue stress because of restricted size and/or numbers of birds per cage.

Most pet shops take great pains to ensure the continued health and comfort of their parrots. The dealer's attitudes to the birds are reflected in a clean, cheery environment designed to maintain the birds in good physical and emotional health. The livestock offered for sale is always plump, well plumaged, and saucy, the epitome of

The Barraband Parakeet *(Polytelis swainsonii)* is sometimes called
the Superb Parakeet—an apt synonym because the bird is graceful
and colorful and has a regal manner about it. Superb Parakeets are
rare in this country and, when they are available, they are usually expensive.

Panama Amazons *(Amazona ochrocephala panamensis)* make exceptionally good pets because they are gentle and classed among the top five best talking species. Some view the Panama as having a somewhat colorless personality, however. This youngster, owned by Richard Favorite, is just beginning to talk.

113

health-and-heartiness—delightful birds guarantee to capture the hearts of young and old. Such pet shops are a pleasure to patronize.

There are a few pet shops, however, which can only can be described as pigsties. Bugs and filth abound everywhere. Birds are purchased at bargain basement prices and sold as healthy birds. Cages are filthy and, just as the bird's environment fails to meet the minimal sanitary conditions one would expect, birds are treated in a lackadaisical manner at best, and roughly at worst: the entire atmosphere, environment, and business ethics are contemptuous of consumer trust. Why the public continues to patronize such pet dealers has never ceased to be a source of amazement to this writer. Fortunately, only a very small minority of pet shops fall into this category, and even that small number is becoming smaller all the time.

A pet shop whose standards of sanitation, treatment of birds, and respect of consumer confidence are abominably low is a business which is best when it is avoided. And, when leaving such a shop, make sure the hands are washed before touching another bird.

Again, a brief synopsis of the things to look for are as follows:

1. What is the general physical appearance of the parrot? Its behavior? Is it animated?
2. Is the parrot plump, a good candidate for a Sunday dinner? Or is it emaciated and thin?
3. Does the parrot show signs of being weak? Does it sit motionless even when threatened? Sit on the bottom of the cage?
4. What are the color of the bird's droppings? What is the consistency of the droppings?
5. Are the feathers ruffled?
6. How does the bird breathe? Spasmodically? Wheezing? Coughing?
7. Are the parrot's nostrils clean or are they plugged up?
8. How are the bird's eyes? Are they fully or partially closed? Are the feathers around the eyes wet and matted?
9. Does a wing droop?
10. What are the conditions in the pet shop? Clean, airy, and sunny? Are the parrots confined to and crowded into too small cages? Overcrowded?

Chapter 6
Buying Your Bird

The retail price of any given species of bird at any given time will differ substantially depending on a wide set of circumstances. Casual comparative shopping will soon reveal that not only do exotic birds differ in price from one pet shop to another, but from one season to another. The differences in price may vary from just a few to several hundreds of dollars.

Retail prices are directly related to a given bird's availability and to consumer demand for birds in general and a given species in particular. When popular demand for a species exceeds the available supply, prices remain high with minimal variance in price from dealer to dealer.

Various species of birds are in short supply for a variety of reasons. While serious attempts are made to breed exotic birds in captivity, some species either refuse to nest, or if they do, they reproduce in such low numbers that breeding programs have a negligible effect on market prices. In most cases where there is a limited success in breeding programs, the cause is primarily found in the breeder's inability to devise a comparable environment to the bird's wild haunts, which is a prerequisite to providing the birds with enough living space free from stressful contact with human beings. When some modest success may be achieved in a breeding program with a particular species of parrot, particularly the larger and more expensive species, the nestlings are generally hand-raised and as such capture premium prices when sold.

But some species of birds have acclimatized themselves exceptionally well to breeding in captivity. Cockatiels, budgerigars, and lovebirds are good examples of successfully bred exotic birds. Indeed, not only did these species prove prolific breeders in captivity, thereby providing the pet industry with a marketable bird

Green Winged Macaws can prove to be exceptionally gentle birds. This young fellow named Rocky is probably the gentlest macaw the author has ever seen. Never having received any formal training sessions, Rocky readily adapted to human contact within one week of ownership. Rocky loves to be cuddled. His owner is Richard Favorite of Norwalk, California.

Opposite:
The Chestnut Fronted Macaw *(Ara severa),* commonly called the Severe Macaw, belongs to a group of macaws referred to as dwarf macaws. Their overall length is generally about twenty inches, the tail making up much of that length. While the Severe is a rarer species than many other macaws, it is still surprisingly inexpensive. They can be reasonably good pets, but once they reach adulthood the best that can be expected of them is a bare tolerance of people. This Severe Macaw is owned by Norma Robinson of Newport Beach, California.

117

which could be mass produced to meet the consumer demands of even the poorest household (and in which mortality rates could be minimized with scientific breeding programs), but domestic breeding programs have resulted in the development of a wide variety of colorful strains as a result of selective breeding. Unfortunately, however, most species fail to breed well in captivity, and therefore large numbers of various species of exotic birds must be annually captured in the wilds in order to meet consumer demand.

The prices of many species of exotic birds are tempered by environmental and political considerations. As tropical forests recede before civilization's advance, the natural habitat of any given species is reduced proportionately. All species of animal life, man included, require what is known in the biological sciences as 'life space'—that is the amount of territoriality required by any given individual, pair, or group essential to its normal feeding and breeding behavior without undue stress being placed on it as a result of overcrowding of that species.

When the life space of individual beings is reduced because the population exceeds the available land and water resources, even when there is an abundance of food available for all, the overpopulation will result in increased stress, fewer mating pairs, and therefore a reduced reproduction rate of the overall population until the population balance—and the life space —is brought into harmony with the species' biological requirements. As habitat recedes before civilization, the life space requirements remain the same, but as the amount of territory available to the species diminishes, the population dramatically decreases. By reducing available habitat, the number of successful matings decreases proportionately. A good example of a species decreasing in number as a result of the reduction of habitat is the Hyacinth Macaw.

The Hyacinth, which is found in the Amazon River tropical forests, is a highly prized bird because of its beauty and temperament. The territorial area required to satisfy its life space requirements is extensive. As the forested area decreases in acreage each year, the number of mated pairs decreases accordingly. But the problem is compounded by another important reason: as prices have risen because of the shortage of these birds, poverty-ridden Indians and peasants search out trees where Hyacinths are nesting. Since Hyacinths nest in exceptionally tall trees, the bird

118

This is a Hyacinth Macaw *(Anodorhynchus hyacinthinus).*

Goffin's Cockatoo *(Cacatua goffini)* is a beautiful cockatoo found on a few islands in Indonesia. Recently, large numbers have been imported and quarantined in California. They are presently among the most inexpensive of all the cockatoos available to bird fanciers, but even so these lovely birds have not become popular. These specimens are from the Busch Bird Sanctuary in Van Nuys, California.

Opposite:
Because of its color, the Scarlet Macaw *(Ara macao)* is probably one of the most unforgettable of the macaws. Its range stretches from Mexico through Central America and deep into Brazil. While the Scarlet Macaw was at one time a relatively inexpensive macaw, it is now one of the most expensive. Scarlets can be gentle pets and good talkers. The bird shown is owned by Lynn Lorenz of Santa Ana, California.

hunters resort to chopping down the tree as a means of getting nestlings. The fact that some young chicks—if there are any yet hatched in the nest—may be killed when the tree is felled is of little concern. The hope that one or two chicks will survive the fall is sufficient enough reason to chop down the tree, particularly when the surviving chick may command the equivalent of a month's salary for someone living at a marginal level of existence.

Because of encroachment on wilderness areas and over-harvesting of wild birds, various governments have enacted conservation measures designed to protect species from over-exploitation. Conservation measures also designate the age of maturity before young birds can be harvested. Mexico, for example, prohibits the harvesting of Amazon nestlings and severely penalizes unlicensed livestock dealers trafficking in birds. It is often said, too, in this regard, that Mexican conservation laws are designed to uphold the high price of Amazon parrots by withholding sufficient numbers from exportation.

The question of supply is therefore an important consideration determining pricing practices. But supply is also directly related to a species' nesting periods. Young birds are always preferable to older birds because they are less prone to die from stress resulting from handling and transportation and are more receptive to training; but younger birds are only available during certain months of the year. Birds of the Cockatoo family, for example, breed during the autumn months, which is the nesting period in the southern hemisphere. Young cockatoos reaching the North American market therefore arrive during the early spring to late summer months. Birds harvested during the autumn, while still young, are not quite as desirable as those harvested earlier. Amazons, however, depending on the species, are found as far south as Argentina and as far north as northern Mexico. Depending on the species and the extent of its geographical range, various young Amazons and macaws are harvested as early as February and as late as August.

When the young birds of a species begin arriving in the pet shops, their prices often drop dramatically. Supply may exceed demand because several quarantine stations at one time may be importing the same species. As the supply decreases, the price begins rising. Mexican Double Yellow Heads during the height of the season often retail at low prices. But at Christmas, when there are few birds available and those that are are no longer really young chicks, the retail price may be almost four times as much.

The question of supply and demand is also determined by a variety of other considerations. The nesting period may be shortened because of drought or prolonged spring rains, thereby affecting the number of successful nestings. Diseases may ravage an area, killing thousands of birds. Because of a shortage in food supply, there may be a higher than average mortality of chicks so that rigid harvesting quotas may have to be established. Some species are less prolific than others. Man-made environmental blunders, such as those caused by extensive DDT overusage, may cripple birds' reproductive capacities and cycles. Quarantine stations may suffer an outbreak of any number of critical diseases which may decimate the quarantined birds at a time when few others are available. Changes in the U.S.D.A.'s quarantine policies may make it more difficult for importers to import exotic birds or import specific species, as happened during late summer of 1978 when stringent policy changes were made making it pro-hibitive for various smaller importers to remain in business.

Whatever the case, bird prices in American pet shops reflect the realities of a variety of variables existing outside of the United States. Bird pricing, moreover, is further shaped by the individual policies of international brokers, importers, jobbers, and pet shop proprietors. Some international brokers may withhold a species from export until demand drives prices upwards, particularly when supplies of a species are limited; the importer, of course, passes the added cost on to livestock dealers.

In a few odd instances, unscrupulous operators have been known to dump a large number of sick birds on the market at bargain prices in order to recover their investments before the birds die. Dumping sick birds on the market to be sold at extreme-ly low prices, while having an immediate effect on legitimate pric-ing structures because the unwitting public buys them mistakenly as healthy birds, does not determine pricing practices over the long run, however.

Finally, competition being what it is, a pet shop owner retails his bird stocks at what he perceives is a fair margin of profit.

This Patagonian Conure *(Cyanoliseus patagonus)* is closely related to conures of the genus *Aratinga*. Conures closely resemble macaws primarily because of their lengthy, tapering tails, their large beaks and heads and the slender shape of their bodies. There are almost fifty different species of conures with virtually dozens more subspecies. Conures can be found from Mexico into northern Argentina and Chile. The more commonly found conures in the United States are the Patagonian, the Nanday and the Halfmoon. Conures can be affectionate pets; some do talk, but most are somewhat noisy birds. This Patagonian is owned by Laura Gibbons of Balboa, California.

Opposite:
The Orange Fronted Conure *(Aratinga canicularis)* inhabits western Mexico. The Orange Fronted is also called the Halfmoon or Petz's Conure.

Usually, a 'fair margin of profit' is generally at least 100% over cost. While such a profit may seem exorbitant, it must be maintained because if birds die, the dealer has suffered an unrecoverable loss. And should the bird be healthy but for some reason fail to attract a buyer, he may have to feed the parrot for as long as several months before it may eventually be sold. Although the cost of feeding birds is marginal as compared to other kinds of livestock, labor costs, medicines, and other expenses incurred in the upkeep of the bird rapidly lower the margin of profit. Added to these expenditures are the fixed overhead costs of rent, electricity, insurance, and so on.

Given that every pet dealer has these operational expenses, bird prices still vary from shop to shop, with the variance often being substantial in some cases. On a recent and rather unscientific survey of seven pet shops in Orange County, California, for example, African Grey Parrots were offered for sale as low as $325 and as high as a whopping $850. In each instance, the birds were healthy but still wild. Judging from the location of the pet shops covered in the survey, it appears that there is a tendency for some stores located in areas with considerable consumer traffic to have lower prices than their more isolated competitors. While these findings would suggest that a bird should be purchased from a pet shop that is successful in maintaining a high stock turnover, caution should be exercised especially when the store does not offer guarantees and is not particularly recognized as a reputable livestock outlet. A pet shop turning its bird stock over rapidly has not had the birds any length of time to determine whether they have fallen prey to ailments once released from quarantine. If the birds are falling sick and are sold just a few days after the birds have been acquired fresh out of quarantine, it is the consumer which will inherit the problems, and perhaps even the death, of such birds.

SOURCES FOR BIRDS

Pet shops are the usual source for most of the birds purchased by the average consumer. Usually located in a neighborhood shopping mall or shopping district, they are convenient to the consumer doing his everyday shopping. Enough of the advantages and disadvantages have been discussed throughout this book to discourage further discussion about pet shops at this point. Suffice it to say that the majority of pet shops are reputable businesses and should one prefer to patronize a pet shop in preference to other sources, comparative shopping will result in a healthy bird of one's choice at some savings. But for those who wish to make a sizeable investment in an exotic bird and who would prefer to thoroughly explore the various kinds of outlets offering birds for sale, there are a number of avenues available before making the final purchase which could result in possible savings in the hundreds of dollars.

Pet columns in the classified ads of a local newspaper are often a good source for exotic birds. Birds are offered for sale by hobbyists, amateur breeders, vest-pocket dealers, and pet owners wishing to dispose of a bird. While many of the exotic birds are sold for legitimate reasons which are in no way connected with the quality of the bird, the buyer should be as cautious as he would if buying from any other source: since birds are often sold through this medium to an unsuspecting buyer because they are either ill or incorrigibly untamable, the bird's health and disposition should be thoroughly examined before the final transaction is concluded.

Sometimes a prospective buyer will find advertisements placed by vest-pocket dealers, hobbyists, and amateur breeders who finance their own expensive exotic parrots by selling birds from their home. Bargain prices for quality birds can often be realized. Some of these livestock dealers sometimes purchase birds in bulk from either a quarantine station or jobber and then retail them at a minimal margin of profit. The buyer should be wary, however, for although prime birds may be purchased this way at a fraction of the cost one would normally pay in a pet shop, many birds offered for sale are second-rate birds which are acquired on an 'as is' basis—that is, birds dumped on the market. Sometimes, too, especially in the states bordering Mexico, such birds are smuggled birds that have undergone considerable stress.

In addition, the buyer can sometimes encounter a hobbyist who is a walking encyclopedia of avian knowledge and who is willing to share his expertise with his customers. Such enthusiasts, because of their extensive contacts, are able to locate a particular species of parrot at considerable saving whose health and disposition is impeccable.

There are nine subspecies of *Amazona ochrocephala*, commonly referred to as the Yellow Fronted Amazon or the Yellow Crowned Amazon. Differences among the subspecies are based on size, amount and placement of head coloring and various other physiological differences.

This trio of Spectacled Amazons *(Amazona albifrons)* had just been tamed at the time of this writing. While not as outstanding in personality as some of their more expensive cousins, they have proved to be personable parrots. They spend a good part of their day chirping to each other and pretending they are still in a viable flock.

Bird farms are another excellent source for exotic birds. Many bird farms, besides breeding exotic birds, operate quarantine stations as well. Because bird farms are usually quite extensive in size and may have dozens of different species offered for sale, a trip to a bird farm is worth the experience itself. The prospective buyer not only has a wide assortment of different species available to him, but prices are frequently lower than at neighboring pet shops. Finally, many bird farms have successful breeding programs so that the buyer is able to buy a legitimately hand-fed chick, depending on the breeding programs that are the farm's specialty.

Another good source for exotic birds is the quarantine stations themselves. Not all quarantine stations retail to the public, however, but some do. When dealing with a quarantine station, the wise buyer will have decided beforehand which particular species he wants, because most quarantine stations which do not operate in conjunction with bird farms will have only a limited number of species at any given time. The direct advantage of buying from a quarantine station rests in the fact that once birds have cleared the quarantine period, the buyer frequently has available to him hundreds of a given species to choose from. By doing one's homework and knowing what to look for in health and disposition, the buyer has the opportunity of choosing the exact bird in prime health. It should be noted that while some importers will dispose of sick birds on an unsuspecting public, most importers are ethical businessmen who would not sell a bird if it were ill. Finally, if there is no urgency in purchasing a bird, and the buyer has had limited opportunity to locate a good specimen of a given species, a few telephone calls to quarantine stations known to retail exotic birds to the public will soon provide the determined buyer with information as to when the next shipment of that species can be expected.

Finally, for the diehard bird enthusiast membership in a local avian society is an excellent source for locating healthy, prime, exotic birds.

The buyer should expect, however, to pay premium prices, for breeders normally cull their stock of ill and deformed birds. In other words, don't look for any bargains. Of no less importance, of course, is the value of membership which broadens knowledge and personal relationships as a result of the various activities associated with the organization.

Of course, not every bird fancier will find it convenient, or even possible, to join a local avian society. Many aviculturists live too far from the societies' meeting places—and many are simply not "joiners."

GUARANTEES

Most livestock sales of one sort or another are almost always accompanied by some sort of verbal or written guarantee concerning the animal's health or pedigree. In some cases, the seller may guarantee the animal free of specific diseases and provide the buyer with documentation that the animal received various inoculations over given periods of time. The purchaser is assured that the animal is free from crippling diseases, is in good health, and that should the animal die within a specified period of time, some form of restitution will be made whether it be a full refund or, as is the case most often, partial compensation towards the purchase of a new animal.

With the sale of exotic birds, however, few such guarantees exist. Birds are constitutionally more fragile than mammals. And, unlike other types of livestock such as dogs, cats, cows, and so on, most exotic birds are not bred in captivity; they have been captured wild and transported while wild to this nation for resale through diverse pet shops. Many of these birds are either adolescent or fully mature specimens that, totally terrified by men and unaccustomed to man's civilization, do not always adjust well to captivity. While most exotic birds do eventually adapt, others are unable to overcome the shock associated with capture, handling, transportation, and confinement. For such individual birds, the resulting stress is sufficient to alter the bird's eating habits so that it refuses to eat the foods placed before it; often the shock is compounded by the fact that the foods are alien to its customary diet. This inability to rapidly readjust and resume normal eating habits results in lowered resistance to the various kinds of diseases that can affect birds. In fact, it is often said that at least one bird dies during the transition period between capture and eventual place-

Leadbeater's Cockatoo *(Cacatua leadbeateri)* is a rare bird in collectors' circles. It is rarely offered for sale, and when it is available, it commands a very high price. These beautiful birds are native to Australia. This fine specimen, caged for breeding purposes, is at the Busch Bird Sanctuary in Van Nuys, California.

Opposite:
There is always some confusion when it comes to the Sulphur Crested Cockatoos. Americans tend to categorize them as Lesser, Medium and Greater Sulphurs, when in reality there are only two types: Lesser Sulphurs *(Cactua sulphurea)*, of which there are six subspecies including the Citron; and Sulphur Cresteds *(Cacatua galerita)*, which include four subspecies. This Lesser Sulphur *(Cacatua sulphurea occidentalis)* is an exceptionally tame and gentle bird owned by Steven Herried of Huntington Beach, California.

ment in a home for every bird which survives the trauma. While this writer has found no statistical evidence supporting this belief, experience in the livestock industry would suggest that such a heavy mortality rate may not be too far from the truth.

Dealers of exotic birds are aware of this fragility and, because most of them are ethical dealers, they stock their avian sections with birds which have demonstrated an ability to rapidly adjust to captivity. They choose birds which have good health and good plumage. They reject birds which, while otherwise appearing generally healthy, show signs of possible illness beginning to manifest themselves. In stocking their stores with healthy birds, they not only perpetuate their own ethical reputation, but they provide greater assurance to future pet owners that the bird is a prime and healthy bird and that given the right care it will continue to enjoy good health.

But no pet shop can accurately predict an owner's treatment of that bird given its fragility. And, regardless of how scrupulous and concerned the pet dealer may be when he buys birds for resale, the birds will still undergo varying degrees of stress in the final transfer from store to home. In this transfer, it is safe to say that the wilder the bird, the greater the stress. Additionally, over-zealous pet owners may place the bird under even greater stress by subjecting it to considerable overwork in its taming and training before the bird has had the opportunity to totally adjust to its new home and master.

This kind of additional stress may be just enough pressure to dramatically alter a bird's otherwise normal feeding behavior and emotional state. If that bird has been exposed to some disease in the past which now lies latent in its system, the drop in food intake and the consequential lowered resistance to disease and infection may be just enough impetus to transform that latent disease into its manifest form. Psittacosis is such a disease. A bird may have been exposed to it, treated for that exposure, given a clean bill of health by a veterinarian, and then suddenly recontract the disease, dying from it because of stress factors resulting a year later when a cat traumatized the bird.

In this connection, just as importantly, most bird fanciers have little understanding of bird health. Because they lack the basic skills essential in assisting a bird to recover from minor illness and stress, a bird's health may progressively worsen without adequate care.

For these reasons few bird dealers are prepared to offer customers the kinds of guarantees often associated with other livestock. When a guarantee is offered, it is usually so short-termed and restricted that in effect it really offers little assurance to the customer. For example, a typical guarantee will provide the customer a full money-back refund should the bird die within the first twenty-four hours of ownership; should the bird die anytime after that, usually only during the first week, half the purchase price is credited to the purchaser, but only if a new bird is purchased. There are other guarantees, some better and some worse, but all of them are basically variations of the stipulations in the above example.

If the parrot enjoys reasonably good health, the chances are extremely remote that it will die within the first twenty-four hours; and if that same bird is subjected to excessive stress so that secondary complications result, the sickness or disease may not be evident for as long as several weeks after.

There are some things, however, that the customer can do to ensure himself that the specimen he is buying will be as healthy as one would expect under the best of guarantees. First, a bird enthusiast should become thoroughly familiar with the kinds of tell-tale symptoms which indicate a bird is in poor health. Second, he should purchase the bird from a reputable dealer. Third, if in doubt about a bird's health, he should make the sale contingent on a clean bill of health from a reputable veterinarian. Any livestock dealer anxious to conclude a sale and confident in the good health of his birds will agree to such an arrangement. Finally, he should provide his new bird with ample opportunity to fully adjust to his new surroundings before subjecting the parrot to strenuous training.

By following these basic principles, a bird enthusiast will feel comfortable with his purchase. For, unlike an automobile, once a bird dies, it dies. There is no replacement of parts. The customer can be a loser of hundreds if not thousands of dollars. And should a parrot require veterinary services, the costs can be expensive. Tweedy Bird, our adorable cockatiel, had to have a gangrenous toe amputated; the total bill, which included amputation, medicines,

Maximilian's Parrot is one of the four subspecies of *Pionus max-imiliani*, a species given by some authorities the common name of Scaly Headed Parrot. Although the Scaly Headed Parrot is common in the wild in Argentina and Brazil, it is not common as a pet in the United States. The bird shown has a pleasant disposition and is owned by Norma Robinson of Newport Beach, California.

Opposite:
The genus *Trichoglossus* includes some of the more popular and colorful lorikeets. This is the Scaly Breasted Lorikeet *(Trichoglossus chlorolepidotus)*, which inhabits Australia.

and two days of recovery and care at the animal hospital, cost $42.19—far more than she had cost us originally.

The best guarantee is to know your birds and your dealer.

BUYING A TAMED BIRD

Buying a parrot which is already tamed, and perhaps even trained to talk or to perform various tricks, can often provide the bird enthusiast with distinct advantages he might not otherwise enjoy should he have purchased a bronco (wild) parrot. Obviously, much of the guesswork in choosing among healthy parrots has been eliminated, insofar as in all species there are some individual birds which are incorrigible and totally untamable because of age or personal disposition. And, when an adult parrot is wild, there is just no way of immediately assessing that bird's potential tameness or talking ability.

A parrot already tamed demonstrates to the prospective buyer that it has the quality of being flexible and that it is capable of entering into a working relationship with human beings. This is an important factor should one wish to teach the bird tricks at a later date. A trained bird reveals that it is a unique specimen within that species, a bird which stands out amongst his fellows. Finally, while not always true, a parrot which demonstrates its adaptability to taming and training is a bird which will be inclined to accept its new masters. There are specific behavioral and character qualities about the bird which normally remain with the bird, irrespective of who the owner may be, unless of course, the bird is abused.

A tamed, trained, or talkative bird is therefore superior to bronco parrots in the sense that the bird has proven itself. Broncos have yet to prove themselves, and many of them cannot. Of course, a proven parrot is more expensive than its bronco counterpart. As an incidental note, this author is familiar with an advertising agent who has been the owner of parrots for several years, his preference being for Yellow Crowned Amazons of the Tres Marias Islands subspecies. Priding himself on his ability to tame parrots and develop extensive vocabularies in them, he went through seven Tres Marias before finding a specimen which proved itself able to learn words quickly. It was a rather costly and time consuming project, but he eventually purchased a bronco which

138

fit his standards of talkability. When buying a tamed bird, this type of guesswork is eliminated.

Unfortunately, many first-time parrot buyers will reject a parrot which has already proven itself in preference to a bronco. Quite often the proven parrot is rejected because it is more expensive than the bronco. Sometimes the rejection results from a matter of pride in that the bird fancier wants to prove to himself that he can tame and train the parrot. Many of these bird fanciers rejecting proven parrots for broncos will suffer considerable disappointment because the parrot may just not meet expectations. As emphasized earlier, there are no guarantees regarding any species. And, while one can reduce the odds of buying a parrot which may fail to meet its species' reputation for a given quality to a negligible level, there will always be an element of risk.

As in the case of pre-fledging youngsters, tamed parrots may seem to be one of the better alternatives when looking for a certain species because of a specific reputation that it may enjoy. While that assumption is correct, there are nevertheless some pitfalls to be wary of when purchasing someone else's tamed parrot.

Human beings become intensely attached to their possessions. This is no less true of their pets. Indeed, one could easily argue that people are even more attached to their pets than to inanimate objects because pets can provide companionship, affection, amusement, cheer, protection, and a host of other qualities which make our lives richer and more meaningful. It is not uncommon to hear of someone who has had a cat or dog which is senile, suffering from deafness or blindness, which would best be put out of its misery, pampered and kept alive often at great expense and personal sacrifice because the pet was 'a member of the family.'

Because people become attached to their pets, they are reluctant to part with them, and when one is offered for sale, there is usually a compelling reason. Generally, of course, the reason(s) are perfectly legitimate. The owner may have developed an allergy to feathers; the neighbors may be complaining about a parrot's screeching which would result in an eviction; the parrot may have taken a disliking to a family member, even though it may be exceptionally affectionate to strangers; getting married to someone who intensely dislikes parrots; getting transferred to the North West Territories; and so on.

The Blue Naped Parrot *(Tanygnathus lucionensis)* is native to the Philippines and adjacent small islands. A small parrot, it has beautiful coloring. This particular fellow has a pleasant and cheerful disposition. He is owned by Richard Favorite.

Opposite:
The Red Vented Cockatoo *(Cacatua haematuropygia)* is an attractive cockatoo native to the Philippines. It is one of the smaller cockatoos. The Red Vented Cockatoo has vermilion and yellow feathers under the tail, an attractive feature not visible in this picture. I have not had a great deal of success taming them and making them into gentle pets. These beautiful birds are part of the breeding stock at the Busch Bird Sanctuary in Van Nuys, California.

But often, too, the tamed or trained bird is being disposed of because of an unacceptable quality within the bird itself. That quality is rarely related to the parrot's physical attributes. Almost always the problem rests in the bird's personality and character.

The parrot may have been a pet for several months but had proven itself to be untamable. Sometimes, as with people, animals suffer changes in personality. As a general rule, a parrot becomes 'mellower' with each succeeding month as a family member. The more a parrot is talked to, handled, and fondled the greater its tendency to accept men and interrelate with them. But not all parrots become better pets with the passage of time. Some birds, for one reason or another, become irascible, testy, unpredictable, irritable, biting people often without provocation. Other parrots may have been purchased because of specific qualities unique to the species, and while one quality may be very much in evidence, other qualities are not. The parrot is therefore sold.

A good example is the Mexican Double Yellow Head. It is generally agreed by most aviculturists that Yellow Heads rank in the top three species (Yellow Napes and African Greys are the other two species) for talking ability. But this fine bird also has a notorious reputation. Some Yellow Heads may never talk, but they may be exceptionally affectionate with their masters. Others may prove masters of mimicry but may be totally unapproachable. To find a Yellow Head which is both a mimic and a 'lover' is the exception rather than the rule.

Such birds are either traded to a pet shop or another private party or are offered for sale through one medium or another. When asked why the seller is disposing of the parrot, a legitimate reason is usually provided—e.g. that there is an allergy to feathers in the family. It would be a rare case indeed should the owner risk ruining the possibility of a sale by candidly admitting that the bird attacks the family's three-year-old daughter constantly, tried to peck out grandfather's eyes, and that everyone had become mortally afraid of it. He would focus his sales pitch on the parrot's remarkable talking qualities.

I so clearly recall a Mexican Double Yellow Head, owned by a neighbor, that gradually over the course of several months became increasingly intolerant of any relationship with people. Once an extremely affectionate pet, it had become so intolerant of everyone

142

The Mexican Double Yellow Head *(Amazona ochrocephala oratrix)* is one of the most popular talking parrot species available to North Americans. Many fanciers consider this parrot species the best mimic of all. In general, the Double Yellow Head makes a good household pet, but it is not at all uncommon to encounter individuals which are testy and untrustworthy.

143

Amazona ochrocephala ochrocephala, often referred to by the common name of Single Yellow Head Amazon. Individuals usually are good talkers. The fine specimen illustrated is owned by Keith Pendell of La Habra, California.

The Thick Billed Parrot *(Rhynchopsitta pachyrhyncha)* is native to Mexico, and it once ranged rarely into the United States. It is not often seen as a pet, though it is known to be tamable.

145

in the family except the wife that to introduce a hand into the cage was to risk a severe bite. With considerable reluctance, the family decided to trade that family pet of five years for an African Grey. The trade was consummated with a livestock dealer who maintained that he knew a breeder who would take the Yellow Head. Approximately three weeks later our neighbor discovered that that same bird had been sold to a bird fancier as a bronco Yellow Head. That is, one which had yet to be tamed!

Then there are pet parrots offered for sale whose undesirable qualities are not quite so blatant. They are testy at times and biters only on occasions. The bite may come today, perhaps next week but when it comes, it will be a good one, a bite which is ugly enough to force the owner to dispose of a family pet. Because of the parrot's unpredictability, the prospective buyer may not have the opportunity of becoming a victim during the time of the sale. He sees the bird for thirty minutes or so, either dislikes or likes the bird, negotiates a price, and takes the parrot home only to find that two days later the parrot has attempted to rip off his finger when he has tried to scratch the bird's crown.

The buyer will assume that he has done something to upset the parrot. Perhaps approaching it too fast. Startling it. Perhaps it was ill. After all, the parrot had been absolutely charming just the night before, loving every bit of attention it so easily received from its captive audience.

It is only after a few days, or even weeks, that the realization eventually occurs that the parrot cannot be trusted when with people. It is liable to inflict an injury at the least expected moment on the most vulnerable person. In such cases the owner has few choices available to him. He can physically avoid the parrot and keep it as something to look at or something to enjoy if it is talkative. He can continue to try to develop a physical and emotional relationship with the parrot in the hope that the bird's irascibility will eventually be remedied. Or he can sell or trade the bird. Usually patience eventually evaporates and the owner will follow the latter routine. And another new owner will undergo the same kind of experience after buying the parrot without being informed about the bird's tendency to become mean and unpredictable.

In the real sense of the meaning such parrots lead tragic lives for they rarely find permanent homes. Half tame and half wild, they live in a never-never land. Such birds would be best off if they were set free, but few bird enthusiasts would be prepared to free them because of their value.

There are not many ways that a prospective buyer can protect himself from making such a purchase. When the parrot is obviously incorrigible, or should it become obvious that the parrot does have undesirable qualities, it would be best to forget about that parrot and search out another tamed bird. Too frequently, however, such parrots are offered below the prevailing prices for prime quality tamed birds and the purchaser deceives himself into believing that he will be able to effect positive changes in the parrot. Such possibilities are remote. That is the reason the parrot was offered for sale after being a family pet in the first place.

Should the parrot appear to have all the qualities of a good pet, it is sometimes possible to effect an agreement by which the final sale is contingent on the new owner having the bird for a brief period on an approval basis. While most sellers would not agree to such an arrangement—mostly because should the bird die while in the buyer's possession it would be difficult to recover the value of the parrot—some sellers will agree to such an arrangement particularly if they want a family pet to find a good home.

An honest seller with honest reasons for wanting to sell a family pet may just very well agree to such an arrangement, if asked, and if the buyer expresses some concern, the buyer may be surprised to find the seller agreeing.

IMPORTING AN EXOTIC BIRD

For those readers who are planning a trip overseas, particularly to tropical areas where parrots are indigenous, parrots can be brought back to the United States duty-free providing that certain conditions are fulfilled. The obvious advantage to importing one's own bird is the substantial savings that can be realized. In countries of origin parrots often cost only a tenth or so of their American cost. Some of the most expensive parrots can be purchased at the price one would expect to pay for the most inexpensive American parrots.

Left: The Luzon Racket Tailed Parakeet *(Prioniturus luconensis)*, sometimes called the Green Headed Racket Tailed Parakeet, comes from the Philippines. Racket Tailed Parakeets are considered delicate and are rare. **Right:** The Kea *(Nestor notabilis)* is a New Zealand species which inhabits the mountains of that country. The Kea is known to eat carrion, but it has also been accused of attacking sheep. Despite the fact that there has been no conclusive proof of this claim, the species has been mercilessly persecuted from time to time over the past century.

Opposite:
The female Eclectus Parrot *(Eclectus roratus)* is a colorful contrast to the male, which is predominantly green with red patches. Males have reportedly made fine pets and good talkers, while females are very shy.

An international traveler can import two parrots a year provided that the following conditions are met:

1. The traveler has been abroad for at least 90 days;
2. The traveler has owned the birds a minimum of ninety days;
3. That after purchasing the parrot(s), the owner has had no contact with other parrots;
4. That the parrots are declared at the first American port of entry;
5. That the importer is prepared to sign an affidavit testifying he has complied with these stipulations.

Upon entry, the parrots are inspected by a United States Department of Agriculture Inspector who, if the parrot is healthy, will release the parrot to the traveler's custody. The only other conditions are that the traveler then quarantine the parrot in isolation for thirty days in his own home, and that at the end of the thirty-day home quarantining, the parrot(s) is to be submitted to a USDA Inspector for a final health inspection.

SMUGGLED BIRDS

The growing popularity of exotic birds in the United States has appreciated the price of various species to the extent that thousands of smuggled parrots are brought into the country illegally each year. There is widespread smuggling because the Federal Government has prescribed stringent regulations governing the importation of livestock in order to protect the health of livestock already here from the introduction of foreign diseases.

Smuggling birds into the United States has become an extremely lucrative business. Investments are doubled, tripled, and even quadrupled overnight in the face of possible imprisonment and heavy fines upon conviction if apprehended. Almost all smuggled parrots enter the United States across the American-Mexican border. Many of the parrots, of course, are of Mexican origin, but a great many find their way through Mexico from various countries in the Southern Hemisphere.

In any Mexican border city there are large numbers of exotic birds available for smuggling into the United States. Possession of quantities of parrots, particularly young chicks, is generally in violation of Mexican Federal Laws governing the harvesting and trafficking of parrots and is therefore subject to laws of arrest and prosecution. But the profits are high enough to encourage both Mexicans and Americans to violate the laws of their respective countries.

When Mexican Double Yellow Heads are in season, an American smuggler can purchase large quantities at ridiculously low prices from a Mexican associate who has paid even more ridiculously lower prices for them. Since legal Yellow Heads clearing a quarantine station necessarily are priced much higher, a smuggler having, say, a hundred birds for sale can clear thousands of dollars in profit in a few days. If the parrots are especially young and are of a type protected by law from being harvested until they are old enough to crack their seeds, the profit will be even greater.

Most of the smuggling is done by small-time, get-rich-quick criminals, but it is suspected that legitimate businessmen might be involved at least to the extent that smugglers occasionally try to involve them as confederates in their schemes. Sellers of legal birds, for example, can be approached by smugglers attempting to cloak their illegal activities by trying to obtain from the holders of birds legally brought into the country the documentary papers attesting to the legality of the non-smuggled birds. Having "documentation" for their contraband theoretically would make it much easier for the smugglers to peddle the illegal birds they hold.

Additionally, customs officials believe there is widespread smuggling of another sort. Some importers contract to buy parrots which have been smuggled from countries which prohibit the exportation of various parrots because of the need for conservation. In some cases, the prohibited birds are actually faced with extinction in those countries enacting such export embargoes. The birds are smuggled into a country which permits exportation regardless of country of origin and the numbers remaining in the wilds. The records concerning the country of origin are then falsified and the endangered birds brought into the United States legally.

Every bird lover should be concerned about bird smuggling.

Canary Winged Parakeets *(Brotogeris versicolorus)* are attractive small parrots. Young birds usually become quite tame, and they are not uncommon as pets.

Caiques are unusually colored South American parrots. **Right:** The Black Headed Caique *(Pionites melanocephala)*, about twelve inches in length. *Below:* White Bellied Caiques *(Pionites leucogaster)* are about nine inches in length.

The restrictions enacted by the United States Department of Agriculture were put into force in order to protect the poultry industry, the wild birds common to our expanses, and the exotic birds maintained as pets by many pet lovers. Illegal parrots have yet to prove they are free from serious contagious diseases, and since most of them are sold to individuals and pet shops, many people come into contact with those birds and thereby increase the risk of possibly spreading contagious diseases to other birds.

Furthermore, as mentioned earlier, it is generally believed that for every bird which legally enters a pet owner's hands, another parrot has died. The losses must be astronomical when parrots are smuggled, for while great care is taken to provide appropriate conditions to reduce stress when birds are legally imported into the country, such care cannot be exercised when smuggling past border patrol units. The conditions in which birds are smuggled across the border are more than just bad—they are barbaric and inhumane. Birds are concealed in the tire housing, in the trunk, behind door panels, and are even frequently, if one can just imagine, taped behind bumpers and underneath fenders. Some smugglers are so greedy and cruel that they even conceal parrots underneath the hood in the engine compartment. Suffice it to say that many parrots cross the border more dead than alive. Parrots being as fragile as they are, the stress they have endured under such conditions kills most of them within a few days.

Every time a group of parrots from a Latin American country crosses another border making its way to the Mexican-American border, it undergoes similar conditions. It would be safe to guess that for every bird which crosses into the United States—whether dead or alive—another four or five birds may have died en route.

While the losses are heavy, there are enough profits to be made that the smuggling continues. A recent arrest in southern California during the summer of 1978 makes a good example of the type of cruelty that these lovely creatures are subjected to. Approximately sixty miles from the Mexican border in California, a station wagon was stopped for a routine inspection. In the back of the car were 556 Yellow Crowned Amazons of assorted subspecies. The parrots were caged in only five crates—imagine, *five crates.*

154

The smuggler was only approximately an hour from the border and probably only three hours at most from the time the parrots were first loaded into the vehicle. But already, almost half of the parrots had died from shock, hyperthermia, and suffocation!

Worse still, all parrots brought into the country illegally and which are seized by the United States Customs Service are turned over to the U.S.D.A. The birds are then automatically put to death! Because of this procedure, many citizens have been reluctant to inform on smugglers trafficking in illegal parrots.

At the time of this writing, however, there is some discussion of providing for mobile quarantine stations wherein seized parrots can undergo a routine thirty-day quarantine period after which the healthy birds would be auctioned off. Whether the government will implement this proposed measure, however, is still a matter of conjecture.

Every smuggled bird purchased by the public—whether knowingly or unwittingly—contributes to the danger of epidemics, the depletion of the world's wildlife resources because of needless and unnecessary waste of life, continued barbarity in the treatment of wildlife, and the potential loss of several hundreds of dollars because the smuggled pet dies from stress and its complications.

It is not possible to detect whether a parrot has been smuggled or not. Mexico only has eighteen different species of parrots and parrot types, all of which are prohibited from exportation until they are able to feed themselves. When extremely young Mexican type parrots are being offered for sale they are generally illegal parrots, even though there are some successful breedings in American aviaries.

Any bird fancier concerned with birds and wildlife in general should make it his civic responsibility to report to the authorities anyone suspected of trafficking smuggled birds. Every port of entry has an Investigations Branch of the United States Customs. Should a community lack a Department of Customs Office, the Assistant Commissioner of Customs, Investigations Branch in Washington D.C. would be pleased to turn over the matter to an agency which would investigate the charges.

Without a doubt, African Grey Parrots (shown is the subspecies *Psittacus erithacus erithacus*) rank among the best talkers. Greys have stable dispositions, an extremely favorable quality, although they are somewhat colorless in personality.

Opposite:
Pet parrots can be an absolute joy. This is the miniature flock mentioned in the text. While Selsa, an Amazon parrot, positively hates Sylvester, the albino cockatiel, he simply adores Tweedy Bird, the gray cockatiel. Selsa will spend hours preening Tweedy Bird but will always chase poor Sylvester away. Of course, Sylvester and Tweedy Bird are good friends. Selsa leads the way, followed by Tweedy Bird and then finally by Sylvester, to make a perch out of the author.

Chapter 7
Stress is a Bird Killer

In previous chapters the effects of stress on a parrot's metabolism and the relationship between stress and health have been brought to the reader's attention on several occasions. Unfortunately, many first-time parrot owners never totally appreciate the significance of stress and its potentially devastating effects on a bird's health. This failure to appreciate the stress factor often results in the handling of perfectly healthy specimens in such a manner as to ultimately prove fatal to the birds.

Stress is a fundamental fact of life affecting all living organisms from the simplest of bacteria to the mightiest of whales. Man is no less exempt from stress.

Stress can be defined as a condition resulting from a conflict situation in which certain detrimental internal changes can occur within the organism. Often, these changes provide the organism with the means whereby it can adapt to the conflict and therefore survive. Failure to adequately respond to the problem—that is failure to resolve the conflict—can lead to internal changes within the organism which can result in death. Stress therefore has a twofold effect: it can help the organism survive and it can result in its death.

While the stress factor seems uncomplicated and relatively simple as per our definition, the exact nature and therefore danger of this problem should not be underestimated.

We might better fully understand the complexity of stress as it affects human beings. Congested freeways make us irritable, anxious, tense. Loss of employment results in sleeplessness, lack of appetite, anxiety. Unfounded and unfavorable rumors about our daily conduct frustrate and anger us. Being caught in a blizzard while inadequately dressed results in shivering, coldness, a slow-ing down of our responses. Overexposure to the sun makes us dizzy, fatigued, and parched. The list is endless.

All organisms are put 'off balance' when faced with a conflict and they therefore try to regain equilibrium by somehow resolving the conflict. The wild parrot handled by a man for the first time attempts to resolve its conflict by biting a hand or fleeing. The motorist caught in a hopeless traffic jam on the freeway at a time when he is already late for an appointment honks his horn, shakes his fist, or curses, and so on. While the traffic tie-up is not resolved by such behavior, our motorist temporarily feels better.

Not all organisms of a given species will perceive the conflict in stressful terms or in the same intensity of stress. Baby parrots, therefore, unknowledgeable in the ways of men, show little signs of stress when handled. An eight-year-old wild cock Macaw, however, will undergo considerable stress when handled. Each organism's response to stress will vary according to its level of tolerance of conflict. Hence, one parrot cowers when first handled by man, but another parrot bites the hand. One motorist shakes his fist while another lights a cigarette.

In speaking of stressful conditions then, we can quickly understand that each organism and each species will differ in their degrees of tolerance to the conditions of stressful confrontation. When a particular species of bird, for example, shows a great deal of tolerance to stress, such as cockatiels, we say that it is a hardy species, just as we say a man is resilient when he 'bounces back' without serious emotional and physical consequences as a result of a serious setback he may have suffered.

But not all organisms bounce back readily.

Stress is the mechanism by which the organism must internally change enough to develop sufficient resistance to a threat, thereby adapting the creature for self-preservation. *Those organisms which cannot react appropriately, and which overreact, will invariably die, for life is one continuous stressful condition after another.* It can be said, therefore, that all organisms are in a state of continued pressure to adapt.

It is the internal changes within the organism, however, which are dangerous to health and which can prove fatal.

The effects of stress on the biological system are both complex and subtle and not yet fully understood. The general internal reac-

A well-tamed and trained parrot explicitly trusts its master and the kinds of handling it may undergo. This Medium Sulphur Crested Cockatoo shows no distress when picked up with one or both hands or, indeed, even when carried under the arm like a sack of potatoes. This Medium is owned by Ken Fenton.

Opposite:
Lesser Sulphur Crested Cockatoos *(Cacatua sulphurea),* while more temperamental and nervous than their Medium Sulphur Crested cousins, still do make excellent pets. This exceptional fellow, owned by Linda Fenton of Fountain Valley, California, is an absolute sweetheart.

tions to conflict, however, have already been identified in terms of the processes involved. When the wild parrot undergoes the shock of being handled for the first time, its body responds by secreting various hormones into the blood stream in quantities beyond its customary levels.

The reader can understand this reaction by imagining himself confronted by a polar bear while unarmed. Adrenalin and various other hormones flow into our blood stream at an unprecedented rate. Our breathing becomes rapid. Our heart beats furiously. Our blood pressure increases. We may even faint. Nature is preparing us to better cope with the threat.

The abnormal amounts of hormonal secretions in the blood stream result in a second shock, a countershock if you will, adding even further damage to the organism's system should the stressful conditions be prolonged. For example, if we have a headache, we take an aspirin, the component drug eventually being absorbed into the blood stream. If our headache does not disappear, we take more aspirins. If the conditions leading to our headaches are not removed, and we continue taking aspirins over a period of time, we may eventually develop stomach ulcers because our hormonal system will release various acids into the stomach to counteract the aspirin.

When we examine the effects of stress on a parrot, we notice that there are three immediate biological reactions: hyperthermia (overheating), which is easily noticed because the parrot will have wing gap and will be breathing faster; hypertension (abnormally high blood pressure); and hypoglycemia (a sharp decrease in the blood's sugar content). The latter two, of course, are not observable. *All of these reactions, whether they be suffered by parrots or men, can be fatal if prolonged.*

These physiological reactions are nature's way of providing the organism the means by which it will have the endurance and strength to either conquer its adversary or escape from it. The fact that parrots are fragile and that overstress can kill them should not, however, discourage a bird fancier from buying his parrot and from taming it. By using good judgment the stress factor never need be detrimental to health. But if the stressful conditions of training continue beyond the parrot's tolerance levels, the trainer may be courting danger. Just as people with weak hearts and high blood pressure suffer heart attacks when confronted with stressful conditions, the healthiest of birds can be killed if pressed beyond its tolerance (of stress) levels.

The trainer will be aware of the parrot's stress factor because stress will cause the parrot to behave in predictable familiar ways. It may tremble. It may cower. It may scream with terror. It may defecate. It may breathe hard. All of these kinds of reactions may be observed in such a simple act as merely approaching its cage, or they may occur only when the parrot is handled. Obviously, should they begin when the trainer approaches the cage, these early responses should tell the trainer that the parrot has low levels of tolerance and that training sessions should be brief until the parrot has had its tolerance levels of conflict gradually increased to acceptable levels.

Few bird fanciers work their parrot to the extent that the parrot dies within a day or two of the stress resulting from continued contact with the trainer. What usually happens is that the trainer exceeds the bird's tolerance level by a large enough margin so that the normal internal stress reactions in the parrot's body persist beyond acceptable levels. As in our example of our person suffering from a prolonged headache whose cause has not been removed, the parrot's biological system attempts to defend the parrot from hormonal secretions, hyperthermia, hypoglycemia, and hypertension. If the parrot was severely overstressed, it loses its appetite, refuses to eat, and draws upon its fat reserves for energy.

By failing to eat regularly and not eating a sufficient amount as required to meet its daily physical needs, a parrot's resistance to disease rapidly evaporates. If there are latent but deadly viral and bacterial agents in the parrot's system, they may become manifest with the lowered resistance. The parrot could die.

In this connection, it is an axiom that a wild parrot which is seriously underweight, or which is recovering from sickness, should never be put into a stressful situation such as is found during taming. Most such birds just cannot handle it.

No one person can completely reduce all stress factors in the taming and training processes or, indeed, in any relationship that the master may have with the parrot once it is tamed. Conflict is part of the parrot's life, and it is the conflict which eventually results in the parrot becoming tamed.

This Moluccan Cockatoo *(Cacatua moluccensis)*, often called the Salmon Crested Cockatoo, was a very 'hyper' and aggressive bird during his initial training; he was also very wily. On at least two separate occasions he managed to bite the author's forearm to the bone. Like most Moluccans, he has become a gentle creature which delights in giving people kisses. Babe is now owned by Mrs. Linda Fenton.

These young Moluccans, owned by the author, are always full of mischief and curiosity. At the time of this writing they were tamed but still not pets which preferred human company. They are still somewhat easy to spook, as their upraised crests show.

In considering the stress factor, the bird fancier may feel comforted in knowing that his wild parrot has already revealed its hardiness and ability to withstand considerable stress. The parrot has already undergone two previously traumatic experiences which killed many of its fellows. The parrot was caught, handled roughly, kept confined to small cages, and fed strange foods. It survived. It was transported from one place to another, amid noises and frightening experiences. It survived.

Its last major stressful conflict will be the taming process itself. If the parrot is already tamed on purchase, so much the better. If it is still wild, proper judgment will also ensure its survival past this last major stressful hurdle.

In this connection, bird fanciers often purchase a parrot on the condition that it be tamed. The shop proprietor, anxious to conclude a sale, presses the bird in order to tame it as quickly as possible. Within a day or two, sometimes within hours, the bird fancier is happy to take home a docile and tamed pet. Sometimes, though, the parrot has been pressed so hard that it never recovers from the shocks to its system and a week or two later, the parrot dies.

Recently, while visiting a friend owning a pet shop in Los Angeles, a man came into the pet shop wanting to trade a magnificent specimen Red Headed Amazon for a cockatoo. He explained that he had had the parrot for two months but was totally unable to do anything with the bird. He expressed his regret for not having once taken the offer of a young man who promised to tame the bird at the man's home within four hours for $35. The young man was an employee of a large parrot outlet in California and described himself as a bird expert.

That bird was an exceptionally beautiful animal, although it was an older bird and probably therefore would have made a poor candidate for a pet. Fortunately, that gentleman did not put the Red Head in the hands of that 'professional.' It is doubtful that that bird, particularly given its age, would have long survived after a four-hour stressful ordeal in the hands of that 'professional bird expert.'

When taming the parrot, the trainer will soon notice that his pet will display various personality characteristics during the first few minutes of handling. Some parrots are extremely timid, others are hyperactive, and still others are hypersensitive. These kinds of personality characteristics must be taken into consideration when taming the bird and eventually training it. We once had a lovely Moluccan cockatoo which we named Babsy. A bronco when we purchased her, she proved extremely difficult to tame. Her initial tolerance to handling was for no more than four to five minutes. After only two or three minutes of contact she would defecate, cower, and begin screaming. Unless we could push her past this limited tolerance level, taming her would indeed become laborious. But to push her might very well result in a level of stress which might be beyond her ability to recover.

At first we kept Babsy's training sessions at the four-minute level, after which she would be returned to her cage for two or three hours respite. She therefore had several mini-lessons each day until gradually her tolerance level began increasing. As her tolerance level increased, so was the length of her daily lessons.

By the time Babsy was being taught to accept cuddling, her tolerance level had increased to fifteen minutes or so. She is now such a gentle creature (she was sold to a pet shop where she is now the store mascot) that she will tolerate hours of harassment, touching, and handling by store customers before she shows any signs of becoming 'hyper.'

Another interesting example of a parrot's tolerance level was a Lesser Sulphur Crested Cockatoo which we named Blondi. Blondi would tolerate working sessions lasting from ten to fifteen minutes, but if they were extended beyond that time she would refuse to eat for twenty-four or more hours after that. She would even refuse offerings of corn on the cob, her favorite treat.

Parrots can get along quite well without eating for a twenty-four-hour period. We normally advise people who buy our parrots to always be conscious of their pet's eating habits. If a perfectly healthy parrot with a hearty appetite misses a day without eating anything that is offered it, the master should be concerned. If it goes two days without eating, he should be worried. And if there is no interest in food by the third day, the master should immediately take the parrot to a veterinarian. Most birds will lose up to one third of their body weight within five days if they eat nothing during that period.

We tried reducing her training sessions to a shorter duration and tried increasing the daily number of lessons. The results remained

Cisco is a Finsch's Amazon *(Amazona finschi)*, often called the Lilac Crowned Amazon. Finsch's Amazons generally make good pets because their behavior is more subdued than that of various other Amazon parrots. Cisco, owned by Lindsay Salathiel of Newport Beach, California enjoys accompanying his master on daily walks.

168

This is Rocky again. This Green Winged Macaw will go to anyone and everyone, for people and cuddling are akin to happiness. Here Rocky shares his affection with Donna Rusinko of Norwalk, California. Rocky is owned by Richard Favorite.

the same—refusal to eat. We finally restricted her taming sessions to two a day, a ten minute period during the early morning and another during the late evening. She was able to handle this schedule without difficulty and would eat voraciously between lessons. Of course, it took much longer to train her, but with each succeeding lesson her tolerance level increased and she eventually became a tamed bird like Babsy, although she never did acquire a tolerance level which would permit extensive handling and harassment.

An interesting adjunct to the story about Blondi was that during the first six to seven days of training she was so stressed that she would eat absolutely nothing so long as there was any sign of a human being in the house. She would eat only after everyone had gone to bed and the house was dark.

These examples are, of course, some of the extreme experiences we have encountered in our parrot taming. Most parrot owners will not encounter these kinds of problems. But if a bird with such a temperament is purchased, it can be tamed and trained and made into an excellent pet if sound judgment and patience are exercised and if the parrot is handled within the limitations of its tolerance levels.

It is understandable that most parrot owners should want to tame their bird as soon as possible. The sooner the taming, the more beneficial the relationship between parrot and man. But haste should not determine the pace of taming and training.

In understanding the full implications connected with the stress factor and recognizing the various personality qualities making your parrot unique from all others, the complications resulting from stress need never become a problem.

Chapter 8
Feeding and Caring
for Your Bird

THE FIRST FEW DAYS

A new pet owner is invariably anxious to begin developing a bond with his wild exotic parrot. Whatever the initial reason for purchasing it, the transaction is always accompanied by some feelings of pride and delight. Even should the bird be so terrified of man that it has severely bitten the hand on the first physical contact between owner and bird, feelings of tenderness, compassion, gentleness, and forgiveness are extended the bird.

The owner is anxious to show the bird that there is nothing to fear from him. He goes to considerable lengths to furnish a new cage with playthings and food treats. He pampers the bird. Talks softly to it. Offers it tidbits, often at great risk to sensitive fingers. He treats it as one would treat a newborn infant.

The owner is anxious to teach it new tricks. To teach it to learn to talk. To teach it to accept love and affection.

Such feelings are understandable and good for they are the kinds of human qualities prerequisite if the parrot is to learn to trust man and become an integral member of family life. But in his zeal to demonstrate his love and affection to the bird, the new owner may forget that the bird is wild and can easily be put into a state of stress. It is an organism which has undergone nothing but unpleasantness as a result of its association with man, and it therefore has no reason to relax and trust its new owner regardless of how loving and caring his master may be.

Most people never seem to realize that the parrot is wild and has never had any reason whatever to trust man, *his owner included.* The bird's trust is not given freely just because some one person talks gently to it for an hour or two, offers it some kernels of corn,

The Elegant
Parakeet
*(Neophema
elegans)* is an
attractive bird.
It is, unfor-
tunately, one of
the many lovely
Australian
species that are
unavailable to
bird fanciers
because of
Australia's ban
on the exporta-
tion of native
species.

Opposite:
This Red Winged Parrot *(Aprosmictus
erythropterus)* is sometimes called the Crimson
Winged Parakeet. The male has more red in the
wing than this female.

and then expects to be immediately and completely loved in return. The bird has been wild all its life, and its instincts have governed its relationship with man in the past, just as they govern the bird's behavior in the present. In order for the bird's trust to be gained, and then later its love and loyalty, patience, persistence, and gentleness must always be the primary rules by which man relates to the wild parrot. It is the man who must prove that he is worthy of the bird's confidence. It is the man who must use these qualities to untie millennia of evolutionary processes which have provided parrots with instincts which were essential to their survival.

To briefly recount the history of every captive parrot, it must never be forgotten that the bird was wild on capture when it was forcibly kidnapped from its familiar environment, handled roughly, shuffled from one cage to another and from one station to another, almost always with considerable force, until it eventually reached its final destination. During that entire period stretching from capture to arrival at its final home, it was deprived of its normal types of foods, denied its usual sources of comfort, deprived of all those activities which give birds pleasure, and terrorized from moment to moment by the machinations of man. Incidentally, birds were not handled roughly because their captors were cruel. On the contrary, wild parrots are difficult to manage and the rough handling results from the bird's struggles.

Even at the time of purchase, the bird underwent further traumatic and terrorizing experiences, and all because the bird fancier decided he loved that particular bird and therefore wanted to buy it. Invariably, unless it was already tame, the parrot was pulled screaming and fighting from its cage—a cage, to remind the reader, that was its last refuge against man. It was put into a confined travelling box, transported home amidst the frightening sounds of people talking, engine noises, and city life. At its new home, it was again pulled forcibly from its final refuge, a pitifully small box when compared to the great expanses the bird once enjoyed, and again subjected to a new environment which was again alien, strange, terrifying. A new cage, new sounds, new smells, new foods, and different kinds of activity are not prone to calm an animal accustomed to the unpleasantries associated with a multitude of similar experiences.

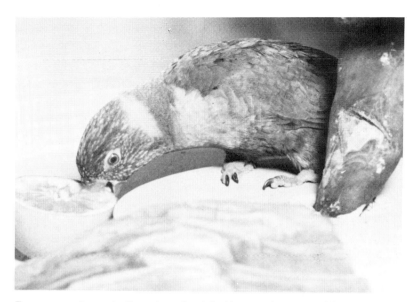

Every parrot needs time to adjust to its new home and become accustomed to its new environment. One way by which you should help it adjust is to feed it the same or similar foods which it was used to eating in the wild. Here a Swainson's Blue Mountain Lorikeet *(Trichoglossus haematodus moluccanus)*, a nectar-eater, has been provided with a citrus fruit.

Such a bird is not the best of candidates who will willingly trust and love his captors.

The first few days for the parrot in its new home are therefore important ones for the bird's physical and emotional health and for the relationship which will develop between itself and its masters. During this transition period, the bird should be given ample opportunity for acclimatizing itself to the new regimen and environment particular to the home and to make itself as comfortable as might be expected under the circumstances where instincts still govern the bird.

Every home has a specific routine unique to itself in which the house bustles with activity during the morning, quiets during other hours of the day, and then bustles again during the late afternoon. The bird needs the opportunity to become involved in that routine and its specific sounds and activities. It needs to become accustomed to the various members of the household going about

Feeding parrots in the morning is always a regular, scheduled activity in the author's household. Here the food cups for the various birds are being prepared. During the preparation some of the fellows like to get into the act. The larger birds normally are discouraged from sampling the goodies because they, more often than not, upset

176

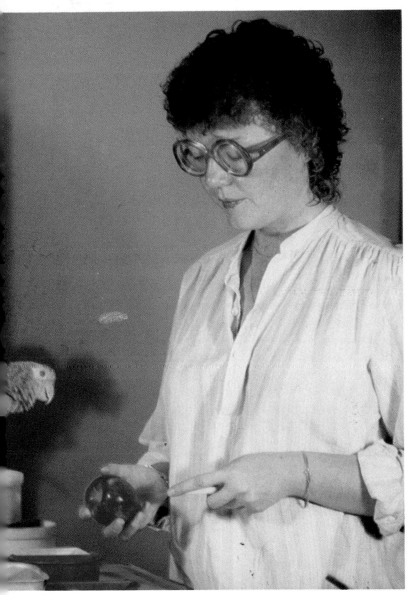

dishes and what have you. A great deal of stress is placed on greens and fruits and, whenever possible, the birds are encouraged to eat these foods in preference to seeds. The diet for the day consists of oranges, grapes, apples, broccoli, Brussel sprouts, bananas, peanuts, almonds, walnuts and some sunflower seeds.

their business in their usual way. It needs to become accustomed to new feeding regimens. In short, the bird needs time to overcome some of its stress and to become adjusted to its new home before any work should be begun with it.

Some birds adjust rapidly, eating heartily within a few hours and more or less tolerating the numerous faces peering at them through the cage bars. Others need more opportunity and time to adjust. It is always therefore a prudent judgment when a new owner gives his new charge a respite from further handling after the bird has been transferred to his final home. From our experience, at least three or four days free from further stress is a good rule of thumb before beginning any physical work with the parrot.

The respite is important for several reasons. Already mentioned is the fact that the bird will have the opportunity to reduce its stress factor and to resume its normal activities of feeding, preening itself, and exercising itself in manners unique to its species. These are important to good health. The respite provides the bird with the opportunity of becoming accustomed to the various household members who will be in daily contact with it. Finally, it will provide the master with the opportunity of assessing its dietary habits, evaluating its personality, and generally exposing the bird to a more balanced diet.

FEEDING THE PARROT

Concerning a parrot's diet, most parrots recently released from quarantine are birds which have had little food variation while in captivity. Most quarantine foods consist of sunflower seeds, corn, or various prepared mashes which are treated with antibiotics. These were certainly not the kinds of food the bird enjoyed in the wilds. In quarantine, the bird eventually becomes accustomed to these foods as its normal fare and when released from quarantine will generally refuse to eat any other. It is important, therefore, for the bird to be weaned from its reliance on these restricted foods and to be provided with a more balanced diet which it will accept.

For the first week or so, or until the parrot begins eating regularly and normally, it is best to feed it only the kinds of food which it has been accustomed to. This can be easily determined by looking in the food trays that the dealer puts into the cages. But remember that although you don't want to change the diet abruptly you might definitely have to change it, because what the bird was eating is not necessarily what it *should* have been eating.

Because of individual differences and the stress factor, some parrots may eat nothing for a day or two after being brought home, while others may start eating immediately after getting food. Whatever the case, it would be best to wait for a few days before beginning a change in diet.

Once the bird has begun to eat regularly again, with patience and persistence the parrot's diet can be shifted from its over-reliance on sunflower seeds to a wide variety of other seeds, fresh fruits, and vegetables. The emphasis must be placed on *patience* and *persistence.* Too many bird owners attempt to change the bird's diet, and after two or three days of failure give in to the bird because it has refused to touch the new foods placed in its dish.

Since a parrot is a creature of habit like its master, its habits, I suppose, could always be broken by submitting it to slow starvation. An 'eat what I put before you or. . .' attitude. Scarcely a healthy philosophy for someone who supposedly loves and understands his parrot. And, of course, to submit to a parrot's one-track-mindedness about what he will eat and what he won't is just as bankrupt a personal policy as the preceding one. Certainly by understanding the pet and remaining patient, you can gradually persuade the parrot to eat other foods.

The procedure is really quite simple. It is a compromise between the other two extreme policies. The bird is slowly, e-v-e-r so slowly, starved each day.

Suppose the bird will eat nothing more than apples and sunflower seeds, four heaping tablespoons a day, regardless what proportion one is to the other. Once the parrot's feeding behavior is regular, reduce the apple-sunflower combination by one tablespoon, and introduce, for example, a sufficient amount of cauliflower to make up the difference.

It will be soon noticed that the parrot asserts its independence and contempt for the cauliflower by contemptuously ignoring the new offering or expediently throwing it out of the food dish in order to get at its favorite foods. At this point, the parrot's gratitude would appear to be as bankrupt as was the bird fancier's philosophies observed previously.

But if the bird's food intake is four tablespoons a day and it will

The Blue Bonnet *(Psephotus haematogaster)* is an attractive Australian species. It is rarely available in pet stores, although it is sometimes encountered in the care of aviculturists.

Opposite:
The beautiful Red Capped Parrot *(Pur-pureicephalus spurius)* is another example of the bountiful variety of avian life populating Australia.

only eat three because it has rejected a fourth, it will be going to its perch hungry each night. Eventually, out of hunger, desperation, or perhaps even appeasement, it will try the cauliflower. Perhaps it will like it. If our stubborn parrot begins eating it regularly, so much the better.

It may be surprising to learn that most parrots can learn quickly. Once the bird has gotten the idea that the new food is there for him to try, he will begin sampling it. The sampling may consist of nothing more enthusiastic than a simple nibble, but he will try it just the same. He will even develop tastes for some foods for which he would sell his soul, foods which he might have previously rejected in disgust. Our Selsa, poor dear, has unwittingly become a cannibal, for when a chicken is in the oven she is there by the kitchen table waiting for a succulent morsel of white meat!

By introducing new foods into the diet over a two- or three-week period, most parrots can be induced into extending the range of their food preferences. While many types of seeds, greens, and fruits will be rejected, many others will be tackled with the same gusto and relish as was true of the sunflower-apple combination.

By developing a balanced diet for the parrot in this fashion, the bird suffers no real harm, either in short- or long- term circumstances. A small pang of hunger each night is not too traumatic a discomfort. By avoiding a 'do or die' stance, the parrot is not needlessly submitted to stress resulting from a lengthy period in which it virtually starved because it refused to eat the strange foods. By refusing to submit to the parrot's insistence on remaining on its preferential, but limited, food tastes, the master can ensure that the bird receives a balanced diet essential to good health. Everyone becomes a winner.

A good trick which can be employed to convince the parrot to try new foods, particularly if the parrot will accept tidbits willingly from the hand, is to hand-feed the bird tiny scraps of a new food item that the bird may or may not have experimented with. The parrot will almost always accept the offering, but will generally almost immediately drop it after taking it from the hand. Even though the offering may be rejected, the parrot will eventually try chewing it if it is offered persistently enough. In general, the more frequent the offer, the greater the possibility that the food will become an accepted part of the bird's diet. It might be added that this strategy rarely works unless the parrot and master enjoy a sufficiently close enough relationship which encourages the bird to beg scraps of food.

Wild parrots for the most part eat a wide assortment of foods. Bugs, various leaves, fruits, and seeds comprise a bird's daily diet. Regrettably, captive birds do not always enjoy a reasonably balanced diet and as a result many bird owners are forced to put vitamins into the drinking water. We have always felt that a captive bird's diet should closely approximate that which it would enjoy in its wild state.

Aside from smaller birds such as our cockatiels or love birds, we approach the feeding of the bigger birds with the intention that their daily diet should include approximately one third seeds, one third greens, and one third fruits. We tend to give the larger parrots less than a full third in seeds because seeds tend to fatten the bird too much and create the prospect of potential heart attacks. Any bird which remains with us longer than a week is subjected in gradual degrees (as noted earlier) to a diet which will include all of the following items:

Seeds: walnuts, sunflower, pecans, almonds, oats, peanuts*.

---

* Peanuts are exceptionally fattening for parrots and should, therefore, be given sparingly. They have a tendency to build up large amounts of fat around heart tissue. Unfortunately, since most pet parrots do not get much exercise, they tend to have heart attacks when there is an excessive fat build up. We like to give our parrots peanuts more as a treat than as a regular stable part of the diet. We ration our Amazons, for example, to six full kernels a day. Even so, our birds tend to get overweight and we generally have to cut down on other seed supplements in their daily diet.

Peanuts, however, are important to a bird's health. Most parrots like them and should yours not, it is wise to get peanuts or peanut derivative products into the bird's acceptance of foods. As noted before, when birds are ill, they stop eating. This of course is dangerous. Since peanuts are fattening, a sick bird which likes them but which is not eating can be encouraged to eat some, thus preventing rapid loss of weight.

Should your parrot not care for peanuts, there is a simple method one can use to get the bird to accept them and to prefer them over other foods. Since most birds will accept tidbits from the hand even when they are not hungry, take a small piece of bread and smear a bit of peanut butter on it. Most parrots will eventually come to view the peanut butter as a

Members of the genus *Poicephalus* are African parrots which look like miniature Amazon parrots. This is Ruppell's Parrot *(Poicephalus rueppellii)*.

The Orange Bellied Parrot *(Poicephalus rufiventris)* is also known as the Abyssinian or Red Breasted Parrot. These birds are about nine inches long.

Greens: radish tops, potatoes, cauliflower, brussel sprouts, celery leaves, fresh corn on the cob, broccoli, turnips.

Fruits: oranges, apples, grapes, melons, bananas, and fruits such as cherries which are available only in season.

Naturally, not all of these items are heaped into every bird's dish every day. The principle of third portions remains the same, however. Some parrots take a dislike to a given food and so it is usually not included in its daily menu. But whatever fruits or greens are in the house at any particular day can go into the food dishes.

TRIMMING THE NAILS AND BEAK

A parrot's talons and beak are in a constant state of growth during the bird's entire lifetime. In the natural environment, stones, tree limbs, and earth all help to wear down overgrowth to manageable levels so that the bird's eating and perching activities are not detrimentally affected. In captivity, however, such opportunities are limited. Talons can become so long that proper perching and gripping activities can become impaired, and in more serious instances the bird may even suffer a foot deformity. Lack of opportunity to wear down an overgrown beak can handicap a bird's ability to eat properly and to eat all the various kinds of food it is accustomed to and should be eating.

By providing a proper cage environment for the parrot, the bird can be given opportunity to maintain the length of beak and talons

treat and will look forward to it. If the parrot becomes ill, it is then an easy matter to encourage the bird to take tidbits of bread/peanut butter.

Another interesting trick which we have found useful resulted from the one time Selsa was sick. She adores peanuts, but when she was ill she refused everything. Her habit every morning is to be sprayed with a fine mist of water. After spraying she particularly enjoys having a few sprays into her mouth.

When she refused to eat during her sickness, I sprayed her with water as usual every morning. But I had concocted a formula of equal parts water, honey and peanut butter which I poured into another spray canister. After the spraying, she waited for something to be squirted into her mouth, and she got several squirts of the food concoction. By repeating the routine every hour, I was able to keep some food going into her and thereby reduce weight loss.

to manageable and appropriate lengths through its own activities. A good cuttle bone attached to the cage wires will encourage a parrot to rub its beak frequently against it. In addition to wearing down the beak length, the cuttle bone serves a useful function in helping the parrot clean food debris from its beak—an important grooming activity because the accumulation of rotting food on the beak and in the nostrils is an excellent encouragement for bacterial growth. Similarly, hard wood toys and perches, while often destroyed within a few days by the bird's voracious chewing activities, help the parrot to keep his beak both clean and trimmed. Excess talon growth, however, is not effectively worn away in the average typical cage. Therefore, talons may have to be frequently trimmed.

Clipping the bird's nails could be an unpleasant and painful experience for both parrot and owner if approached in a careless and insensitive manner. At least for the first occasion or so, the parrot will probably resist having its nails trimmed until the trimming becomes a routine procedure in its life. The resistance can be accompanied by painful bites if precaution isn't exercised.

But clipping a bird's nails does not necessarily have to be traumatic, frightening, or painful. In preparing to trim the bird's nails, an old towel, clippers, hydrogen peroxide, Qwik-Stop (manufactured by the Animal Research Center and found in most pet shops), and two people are all that is required. Dog or specially designed bird claw clippers are best. Avoid scissors for they are generally not sharp enough to make clean cuts without damaging the remaining part of the talon.

After removing the bird from the cage, it should be placed on the floor or table (or if tame enough, perched on the arm). After throwing a towel over the parrot, the helper should gently grab the bird around the neck from behind, just below the skull and hold just firmly enough so that the confused and frightened parrot will be unable to twist its head around to bite. The towel should then be wrapped around the bird in order to restrict its struggles. It is important to restrict the bird's movements for, aside from the possibility that its fright may lead to a nasty bite, the parrot may not only injure itself by excessively struggling in order to free itself, but the struggles generally result in the plumage becoming disheveled and damaged.

The Long Billed Corella *(Cacatua tenuirostris)* is one of nineteen species comprising the cockatoo group. The Corella and most other cockatoo species are native to Australia. This particular species is rapidly declining in number, a decline which is escalated as lands are converted to pasture and grain production.

Opposite:
This Moluccan Cockatoo has an interesting history. Turned into a neurotic bird because of the misguided training he had received from the husband of a previous owner, he was retrained with considerable effort and eventually became tame enough to tolerate people. After living in a pet shop for a month, he began to show a distinct liking for women and a dislike for men.

Care must be taken
when trimming either
the claws (left) or the
beak (below) so that
the blood line is not
severed. If a bird's
beak grows too long,
it is an indication
that the bird has not
had enough hard
substances on which
to chew.

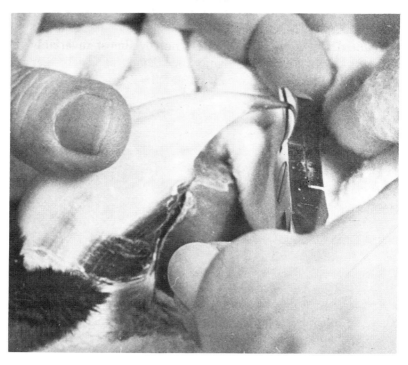

Because the towel will put the parrot in darkness and prevent it from realizing what all the excitement is about, it will quiet down almost immediately after the initial start. If it does struggle, the struggling will be mild and short-lived. If anything, the parrot will contentedly chew on the towel and will not inflict injury to either person or itself. The person performing the trimming can then leisurely hold each leg separately with one hand, prying apart one curled toe at a time from the clenched foot, and appropriately clip each nail at will.

A word of caution, however. Each nail has a nerve which traverses down almost all of its entire length. Depending on the bird's size, and the frequency of nail trimmings, this nerve extends approximately four-fifths down the length of the talon. To clip the nail and inadvertently the nerve at the same time, which sometimes happens, will produce a minor bit of pain, a squawk perhaps, a brief but subdued attempt to renew the struggle, and a renewed vigorous chewing of the towel.

The end of the trimmed nail will seem to gush forth an alarming and what seems to be an unending and copious flow of blood. Even though the parrot remains relatively unconcerned except for the initial few signs of discomfort noted, almost invariably the owner verges on absolute panic and visions of a dead pet put owner and helper into near hysteria, but there is no need for alarm.

The bleeding can easily be stopped by first dabbing the wounded nail with cotton dipped in hydrogen peroxide to prevent infection and immediately afterwards by applying some Qwik-Stop to the injured talon and holding it there for a minute, which will coagulate the blood enough to prevent further bleeding. Eureka! The parrot when released from the towel will strut about bewildered a second or two in getting its bearings, will ruffle and shake its feathers somewhat indignantly at its treatment, and will be no worse for wear or tear.

By keeping the talons trimmed regularly, they can be maintained at a reasonable length as would be the case if the parrot were still in the wild. Importantly, too, there will no longer be the problems faced by the master of long unkempt nails with sharp points gouging into the arm or shoulder and almost always ruining one

Being intelligent, parrots can be trained to perform a wide variety of complicated tricks. All that is required is an analysis of the components which comprise the trick to be learned, patience and a strict adherence to the rules of conditioning.

Opposite:
This pair of Blue Fronted Amazons *(Amazona aestiva)* are owned by Jean Broadhead of Huntington Beach, California. Jean named these birds Sugar and Spice, appropriate names for two mischievious but exceptionally gentle creatures.

good shirt or blouse after another. We clip our birds' talons regularly every four to five weeks or as needed.

The trimming of the bird's beak is not that often required. Indeed, most exotic bird owners may never find it necessary to trim the beak. Generally, because the parrot usually has ample chewing materials in its cage and it usually thoroughly enjoys chewing anything and everything, it will chew every item in its cage into absolute shreds. The first-time pet owner may also soon discover after he has had that first parrot for two or three days that the bird has the unpleasant and somewhat unnerving habit of grinding its mandibles together, particularly at night when everyone is trying to sleep, as if it was some type of maniac deciding in its frustration and aggravation who it will vent its anger against. This is true of even sweet cockatiels. But again there is no cause for alarm. The parrot is simply reducing beak growth by the best way possible—the manner which nature has taught it is the most effective method. Soon, too, what was once considered an aggravating, unpleasant, annoying, and incessant grinding of mandibles will just become another idiosyncrasy that the master will learn to live with without difficulty.

A final note. Once a parrot's talons have been trimmed a few times and the parrot is tamed and sitting on its perch and cocky as a good parrot should be, it is often very easy to distract the bird's attention with some favorite tidbit or head scratching by one hand, while nail clipping with the other hand. Before the parrot has realized what has happened to it, it has had its nails trimmed, its stomach filled, its head scratched, its ego bolstered, and it has been no worse or no wiser for the experience.

CLIPPING THE WINGS

Most tamed parrots eventually become like all other household pets. They will beg for food at the kitchen table, provide companionship for their masters, play games, and in general conduct themselves in a manner which is common to all other animals that have been prized as pets throughout history.

As a parrot becomes less dependent on its instincts for survival and more reliant on its master, its tameness and domesticity become increasingly taken for granted. The fact that the parrot was at one time a wild bird is soon forgotten, at least conveniently shelved away into some dark recess of the mind. And the apparent domesticity of the parrot blurs the understanding that *its instincts still comprise the bird's psychological makeup.*

The newspapers are replete with news items about so-called tamed pets that have renounced their relationships with their masters by either attacking them or fleeing. A little while back a hippopotamus from Lion Country Safari escaped its enclosure, sought refuge in a local pond, and was successful in eluding its pursuers for several days until it was inadvertently killed by them several days later. In a more tragic vein, there was a news story about a snake hobbyist who was strangled to death by his pet boa constrictor, and the Los Angeles *Times* carried a story about a lioness which mauled her mistress to death in Florida.

Of course, exotic birds do not kill their owners. While a pet parrot may neither kill nor seriously injure its master, it is capable of fleeing from captivity. For, after all, wild birds which have been converted to domesticity are nonetheless still wild birds whose instincts still persist under a veneer of domesticity and tameness. Orange and Los Angeles Counties in southern California, where there are probably more pet exotic birds per capita than anywhere else in the world, have numerous flocks of various species of parrots which have escaped and reverted to their wild state after being explicitly trusted by their masters.

Sadly enough, many well meaning pet owners never clip their parrot's wings because of the underlying love and dependency that the parrot seems to have in its rapport with its master. Taken for granted, its continued loyalty and dependency on the master are never doubted. And sometimes, even out of vanity, a parrot owner may reject wing clipping because it supposedly mars the bird's appearance. Unfortunately, too often does an owner take his trusted parrot outside the home or accidently leave a window or doorway open, only to find that the parrot has suddenly taken flight. Away into the wild blue yonder and almost always away for *good.*

We placed a similar trust in our Double Yellow Head, Selsa, which we had acquired when she was barely four months old. We never clipped her wings because my judgment was blurred. "After all, it would ruin her appearance. After all, she's been with us since a baby. After all, she has never ever, ever tried to fly anywhere."

Moluccan Cockatoos are noted for their intelligence, and some prove to be excellent talkers. Most Moluccan Cockatoos are affectionate with people, but some are not; there are marked personality differences among different individuals. The two young males shown here spend hours grooming each other.

This is the infamous Selsa mentioned in various places in the text. She is an absolute darling, but she can be very unpredictable. Not long ago, for example, she bit a ten-year-old child without apparent provocation. Despite her occasional transgressions, she immediately endears herself to everyone.

197

Our habit was to take Selsa with us almost everywhere because she was such a delightful and charming companion. One fine Saturday afternoon when she was approximately a year old, while at an Orange County Swap Meet, for some reason known only to her, she decided she had had enough shoulder riding and launched herself into the air without warning. Assuming an altitude of approximately ten feet, she proceeded to fly northwards.

Because of the trucks, signs, balloons, and what have you characteristic of swap meets, it was difficult to keep sight of her but we ran after her nevertheless, yelling "Selsa, Selsa, Come back." The reader can imagine the incongruous spectacle of two grown adults yelling for the bird to come back when she had totally different intentions.

But all is well that ends well. She flew approximately a hundred yards, falling short of what seemed to be a towering tree, to land on the pavement. A bystander quickly pounced on her. And we, even quicker, chopped off her flight feathers. "Hacked them off" would be a better and more accurate description. After the hurried hatchet work, she looked very, very butchered, but butchered or not she is still ours, even today. Her wing clippings now are as regular as her growth of new flight feathers.

A parrot's wings are covered with two distinct sets of feathers. One set is known as the flight feathers—these are the long feathers along the rear edge of the wing that make it possible for the bird to fly. The other feathers, known as coverts, are rows of smaller feathers that cover the lower third of the quill end of the flight feathers.

In order to restrict a parrot's ability to fly, the flight feathers must be trimmed a certain amount. In shearing the feathers, we prefer to clip just enough of them so that if the bird is gently thrown into the air it will not drop straight downwards for, in doing so, it could injure itself because the bird has lost its ability to break its fall. Rather, there will be enough feathers left to allow the bird to gradually reduce altitude in a downward gliding motion, so that it lands a short distance away on its feet.

There are two schools of thought governing feather shearing. One group of bird enthusiasts prefers to clip only one wing. They believe one clipped wing is preferable to two clipped wings

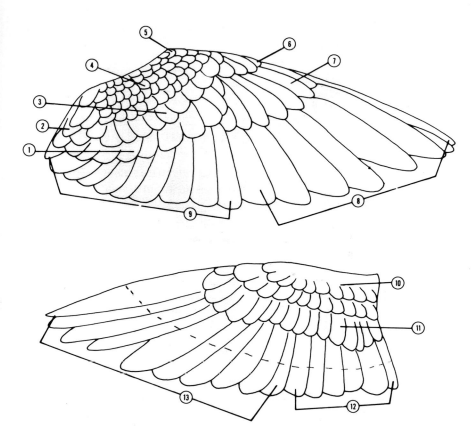

The following are the descriptive parts of a parrot's wing.
(1) secondary coverts, (2) tertials, (3) median wing-coverts, (4) lesser wing-coverts, (5) bend of wing, (6) carpal edge, (7) primary coverts, (8) primaries, (9) secondaries, (10) lesser under wing-coverts, (11) greater under wing-coverts, (12) secondaries, (13) primaries. The line drawn across the under side of the wings indicates the approximate cutting line when only one wing of the parrot is to be clipped.

because first of all, should the parrot be actually able to gain altitude and begin flying away, the loss of air pressure on one side of the bird due to that wing's sheared flight feathers will cause the bird to fly in a circle bringing it back to its point of origin. Hence its immediate capture.

200

Unfortunately, Hawk Headed Parrots, *Deroptyus accipitrin us,* are rare in the United States. These unusually colored birds make excellent, intelligent pets; and they also have bred in captivity.

Opposite:
Although it is also rare to see the Lesser Vasa Parrot, *Coracopsis nigra,* in the U.S., this somberly colored bird is reported to make a fine and intelligent pet.

We have had experience with that school of thought. A colleague of mine one evening brought home a fine full-feathered Moluccan Cockatoo specimen which he planned to deliver to a customer the following afternoon. A fourteen hundred dollar bird. He asked me if I would help him clip the parrot's wings. Not wanting to ruin the bird's appearance, and believing that four clipped feathers would be sufficient enough loss to force the bird to fly in a circle should it escape, he clipped the first four feathers of the right wing and we returned the Moluccan to its perch.

The following morning his five-year-old daughter left the kitchen door open, and the Moluccan sitting on a free hanging perch and seeing freedom beckon, slipped out after her. What happened next is best described by my colleague.

"When he hit the air I noticed that he had a slight drag to his right, for the cockatoo was veering in that direction. Within four or five seconds he had straightened his flight pattern by reducing the strength of the wing beat by his left wing, thereby compensating for the drag on his right. The last I saw of him he was flying straight as an arrow for God only knows where."

Actually, we did encounter that Moluccan again. The bird was reported sighted approximately five miles away in Santa Ana. After a local animal shelter telephoned my colleague to notify him of the sighting, we went to the location on several occasions with the hope of recapturing it. All to no avail. We did see it on a number of occasions but always from a distance. He always made a marvelous sight in the far distance.

To the best of our knowledge that Moluccan still remains uncaptured and still contentedly goes about his business.

Another reason why some bird fanciers only clip one wing is because they feel that when both wings are trimmed there is no opportunity of viewing the fine feathers and colors common to the unclipped wing. At least with one unclipped wing, so the argument goes, one can see Nature's design and colors. Opponents of this one-wing philosophy feel that the bird looks unbalanced when one wing is left intact while the other is sheared. They prefer to shear both wings equivalently, thereby retaining the parrot's streamlined and balanced appearance.

We, frankly, prefer the two-wing approach of flight immobilization. But since most parrots will already be clipped when purchased from the livestock dealer, the reader will be better able to judge for himself which method of wing clipping is appropriate and satisfactory for his aesthetic needs. Should the parrot be unclipped, a pet dealer will be pleased to trim off the flight feathers in whichever manner is desired by the purchaser.

Frequently, quarantine station operators will clip only one wing and unfortunately in most instances that clipping will usually be done in a haphazard and disfiguring fashion. When there are several hundred wild parrots in a quarantine station which must be immobilized so that they can be easily handled, labor costs prohibit careful and time-consuming clipping of each individual bird, even though the entire process per bird may only take two or three minutes. A parrot is grabbed by one worker; its wings stretched out; a second worker snip-snips and the bird is returned to its cage. Sometimes the snip-snip leaves the wing normal looking. Most other times the wing's plumage looks quite unfashionable at best. But the butchery does serve its purpose.

In order to clip off a parrot's flight feathers, all that is needed are two people, a pair of scissors, and a heavy old towel. Qwik-Stop and hydrogen peroxide should be kept handy. Once a parrot has become tamed and has undergone the shearing process a number of times, it will generally permit wing clipping without resistance and struggle and therefore there will be no further need for the towel. But until such a time, it is best to cover the bird with the towel so that it cannot see what is happening to it. As with talon clipping, the covered parrot will probably do nothing more than contentedly chew on the towel while the trimming takes place.

Feathers that are still growing in contain a short blood vessel that traverses the first 10-15% of its length. This blood vessel, of course, is responsible for the feather's growth. Sometimes, when inadvertently trimming the feathers too close to where they are growing from the wing, the vessel is severed and bleeding results. Should that happen, the treatment is simple; first dab some hydrogen peroxide over the wound, and then apply Qwik-Stop to the injury in order to coagulate the blood.

In order to avoid inflicting unncessary injury to the bird during its wing clippings, prudent judgment is required; for larger parrot types, do not clip along the line of the coverts. Make the cut approximately half an inch away from the coverts. With

The Australian King Parrot *(Alisterus scapularis)* is a beautiful bird from Victoria, southern Queensland and New South Wales.

The Princess Parrot *(Polytelis alexandrae)* is a colorful species which
inhabits the arid regions of western Australia.

smaller birds, of course, anywhere from an eighth of an inch to one quarter inch will leave the bird free of injury.

One person should hold the bird gently but firmly around the neck, just below the skull. The bird should be positioned and held firmly so that it will be unable to struggle violently should it become frightened. Once the bird is held securely, the other person then gently stretches out the wing and snips off the appropriate flight feathers. If it is preferred that both wings be trimmed, then it is a simple matter to release the trimmed wing and proceed to stretch out the second wing and repeat the process.

If only one wing is to be clipped, it is advisable to clip off all the primaries of the wing decided upon. If both wings are intended for clipping, then the trimming will depend on the size of the bird, its species, and the manner in which the primaries lay on the back of the bird when the wings are folded. With cockatoos, for example, the first four or five primaries on each end of the wing are clipped off. When the wings are folded against the body, there is no outward indication that the flight feathers have been clipped off. And, should the bird stretch its wing, the resulting gap is not unsightly.

With Macaws, Amazons, and various Amazon type parrots such as conures, the lay of the wings on the back dictates which feathers are to be trimmed away. In order to protect the neat appearance of the wing's plumage it is necessary to leave the first three primaries at the end of each wing and to trim out the intermediate primaries. Hence, leave the first three primaries, trim out the next five, and leave the remainder. Should the parrot still have flight power (this can be tested by gently throwing the bird into the air), trim out another feather on each wing and repeat the testing until sufficient primary feathers have been trimmed from each wing to cause the bird to glide to the floor regardless of how fervently it tries to maintain altitude. Its glide should not take it more than eight or ten feet away. Since there are many different Amazon species alone and each species has its own distinctive wing structure, there is no fast rule applicable to each and every species without resorting to the drastic step of trimming off all of the primaries—an unneeded and drastic step. But by following the procedure noted here, the parrot fancier will soon discover how many feathers must be removed with his particular species of bird, so that there will be no need for experimentation the next time. And the parrot will look as natural with its wings folded as if there had never been any feathers trimmed from the wing.

With some parrots and parrot types, however, almost all of the flight feathers have to be clipped away, as with cockatiels. Leaving a cockatiel with one primary feather is like allowing it ten feet of flight. Leave three or four primaries, and the cockatiel just might fly away. Permanently. With our pet cockatiels, therefore, we trim off all the primaries making sure that in the clipping process we shape the feathers so that the wing looks as natural as can be in the folded state.

BATHING THE PARROT

Nature always takes its own course and tells the various species of life through their instincts what their appropriate behavior should be under any given situation affecting them. But sometimes, while in captivity, parrots lose many of their natural instinctual patterns of behavior. Many captive parrots often do not groom themselves regularly. Others, because their cages are cleaned irregularly, accumulate considerable dirt and body wastes on their feathers. Still others, through no fault of their own, have their feathers dirtied. In each case, the feathers lack luster, are dirty, and are unhygienic to the bird's health.

It is best, if possible, in preference to bathing a bird, to encourage it to clean and preen itself. This habit can often be easily inculcated by providing the bird with a dishful of water in the morning during the cage cleaning and feeding period or by developing in the bird an enjoyment for an early morning spray from a pump sprayer. But sometimes these techniques fail, and the parrot fails to take the initiative in taking appropriate care of its plumage. A bath may therefore be in order every two months or so.

The reader should not be over-cautious about the idea of giving a bird a bath. After all, most parrots and parrot types come from tropical regions of the world where daily downpours are as regular as clockwork.

It is highly recommended, however, that the bird be tamed before it is subjected to a bath by its owner. A wild bird may not take too kindly to the kind of contact that occurs between master and bird during the bathing.

The Masked Lovebird *(Agapornis personata)*, an attractive East African species, is a perennial favorite with breeders. It is hardy and breeds well in captivity. Unfortunately, it is known to have a spiteful disposition and does not lend itself well to becoming a tame pet.

Most parrots love to bathe. Here a Peach Faced Lovebird *(Agapornis roseicollis)* indulges itself in a favorite pastime.

209

All parrots love taking baths. A pan of water placed in the cage provides the bird with an opportunity to play which is essential to good emotional health. Birds also enjoy being sprayed with a fine mist, as in this picture.

The method is to place the pet on a perch in the bathtub underneath the shower. The water running through the spout should be approximately the same temperature as that used when giving a baby a bath, and the flow of water should come downwards in as soft a fall as possible. *Under no circumstances should the water be cold.*

The parrot almost always enjoys the water falling down on it. Once the parrot is soaked (there is not one parrot which does not look absolutely terrible when it is drenched), take a small dab of the mildest baby shampoo possible and with two or three fingers gently rub the shampoo through the bird's plumage. Since the poor fellow is generally too concerned about the water falling on his head and eyes to worry about any other inconvenience, a tamed parrot will offer no resistance to the shampooing.

It is particularly important that the shampooing action of the fingers be as gentle as possible otherwise the plumage will be ruined, at least until the bird molts again.

Allow the warm shower to rinse off *all* shampoo. Remove the parrot from the shower and *pat* it dry with a thick towel. *Do not rub the feathers,* as one would a dog's fur, because the plumage will become absolutely frayed and damaged beyond repair.

The bird must be protected from a chill. Once the excess water has been patted from its plumage, place the parrot on its perch in a warmly heated room. You will need a temperature of eighty plus degrees. We like to keep our bathed parrots in the bathroom where the heat from the shower has heated the bathroom air. We also keep a small electric heater in the room kept safely away from the parrot to reduce possibilities of injury. The parrot will groom its wet feathers, straightening them out and again making itself presentable.

In two or three hours your pet will once again be clean, and within a few short days its plumage will have an iridescent and bright quality to it.

A word of warning, however. A bath once every two or three months is sufficient. If the parrot seems dirty again within a week or two after its last bath, it is probably not the parrot's fault. We have usually found that the principal reason for filthy plumage rests with the master who fails to keep the cage clean and hygienic.

Like other members of its genus, the Regent Parrot *(Polytelis anthopeplus)* has a long tail, a small head and a plump body.

The Dusky Parrot *(Pionus fuscus),* sometimes called the Violet Parrot, is a rare bird which inhabits South America.

Meyer's Parrot *(Poicephalus meyeri)* is native to Africa. It is also known as the Brown Parrot, and the six subspecies show only slight differences in the unusual color pattern.

Bronze Winged Parrots *(Pionus chalcopterus)* are similar to Amazon Parrots in body form, but they are much duller in over-all coloration.

213

THE CAGE, ITS CARE AND UPKEEP

The cage plays an important role in the parrot's life. Aside from a convenient place to house the bird, the parrot perceives his cage as his own particular piece of turf. Indeed, some parrots even show a resentment to any intrusions into the cage. The cage serves as a haven for the bird. It is a place for it to seek sanctuary, food, water and rest. It is a pinacle from which it can survey its limited world. The cage, being as important as it is to the physical and emotional comfort of the parrot should, therefore, be spacious and comfortable enough.

Common sense should tell a bird fancier that a cage should be appropriate to the bird's needs in size and roominess. Too often, however, one sees a larger parrot such as a Yellow Nape cramped into a cage designed for a conure. A caged bird requires ample room to exercise itself and perform its daily routines without being constrained by the size of its enclosure. Even when the bird is tamed and accustomed to coming and going from his cage, it still requires room for maneuverability because a significant part of its life will be spent within the enclosure in pursuit of its feeding and sleeping activities. If in doubt about the appropriate size of the cage when buying one, ask the pet shop attendant for his recommendations. There is a wide variety of cages which are suitable for every type bird sold which can be purchased at reasonable prices.

Prudent judgment should be exercised in stationing the cage in the home. Like man, parrots catch chills and colds, and as discussed earlier, while colds may not be killers themselves, they may lead to complications which could seriously affect the parrot's health. While it is humanly impossible to prevent your parrot from catching a cold, it is possible to reduce the probabilities of that eventuality. All birds should be kept away from drafts, particularly in those regions of the country where climatic changes are common from day to day. While windows are excellent places for a bird to enjoy the sunshine, they are also places where drafts are frequently found.

Some birds are heartier than others and can handle changes of temperatures and drafts without undue danger to their health. But being prudent in stationing of the cage is always a wise policy, regardless of whether the parrot appears exceptionally healthy and hearty. Place the cage in an area of the room where there will be an ample amount of light—sunlight is obviously preferable—and where the pet will not be exposed to draft conditions. A lighted match held near the cage will always help a bird owner to detect whether or not a draft is blowing through the cage. Concerning air conditioners, while numerous bird fanciers expose their birds to constant lower temperatures without seemingly any ill effects, such pet owners unnecessarily expose their parrots to potential health problems.

While a bird's good health is contingent on a variety of factors, it is an axiom that a clean cage is essential in the care of the bird. Dirty cages encourage bacterial growth, mite infestation, and other deleterious conditions which can affect the health of a bird. A parrot which lives knee deep in rotting food and its own droppings is a prime candidate for sickness and parasites.

Cleaning the cage should be as routine as feeding and watering the pet. Simply speaking, food debris and bird droppings should be removed from the cage each and every day. There is no excuse for filth. Unfortunately, many well meaning bird owners clutter their bird's cage with profuse paraphernalia to the extent that the poor creature has little room to find perching space. Toys will indeed relieve some of the bird's boredom, but by over-cluttering a bird's cage it is doubtful that the parrot's boredom is that much better resolved.

By all means give the parrot some toys to chew on and destroy. Should the parrot's interest slacken, toys can be changed from day to day. But avoid over-cluttering the cage area. Give the parrot ample room to climb about its cage at will.

While many bird owners prefer to cover the cage's tray with newspaper, we found it practical and convenient to cover the tray with a quarter inch of coarse grained sand. Such sand, free of dust, can be purchased in many pet shops for ten to fifteen cents a pound. Using a kitty litter scoop, the droppings and food particles can be conveniently lifted out and discarded leaving a sandy clean floor for the bird. Since bird droppings have little or no odor, the sand can be safely kept in the cage for as long as two or three weeks, depending on the size of the bird, although we prefer to replace it every week.

A sand floor has several advantages. It cannot be shredded into pieces like paper. It does not have to be cut or folded to conform to

The Red Lory *(Eos bornea)* is found on a few islands in eastern Indonesia. An attractive bird, it is one of the best known in its genus and is imported regularly by aviculturists and bird fanciers who enjoy collecting.

Opposite:
The Hyacinth Macaw *(Anodorhynchus hyacinthinus)* is among the most beautiful of all macaws. Because of its beauty and gentle disposition, this large bird is eagerly sought after. When pairs are observed nesting in an inaccessible nest in a tall tree, the tree is felled with the hope that any nestling will survive the fall.

the shape of the floor. It is inexpensive and it provides a source of grit for the parrot's crop. And because the sand absorbs moisture, the tray does not need to be scrubbed each day as is the case when paper is used for the larger parrots and macaws. Its principal disadvantage, aside from the fact that it is not free as is true of used newspapers, is that the parrot will often scatter some of the sand outside of the cage during its everyday activities, particularly if the bird is an exceptionally active one.

A good habit to cultivate is the routine of weekly or biweekly cleaning and sterilizing of the entire cage. While it may seem unnecessary to routinely scrub down the entire cage, the small amount of effort expended every few days has a beneficial and healthy effect on both bird and home. Besides usually climbing about the bars of the cage, parrots often spend some of their time on the floor of their cage where they do one thing or another, walking in the food debris and in their own droppings—some of which clings to the feet. When the bird resumes its bar climbing, some of this floor refuse is transferred to the bars, which consequently become soiled, and eventually gets rubbed off onto the parrot's plumage.

To clean and sterilize the cage, dismantle it and remove all toys, food dishes, and perches. The cage should be thoroughly soaked in water for a few minutes and the various items which were removed from the cage should be placed in a bucket of Lysol and soapy water. (Bleach *or* ammonia can be used instead of Lysol). Never mix these chemicals together, as a noxious gas is produced which can be dangerous to one's health. Scrub the soaked cage down with a heavy sponge dipped in the cleaning solution. If the debris is heavily encrusted on the bars of the cage, a wire brush may be needed. The perches should be scrubbed thoroughly with the wire brush and then washed down with the cleaning solution. After rinsing everything off, allow it to dry. Not only will the cage be sweet-smelling, but its appearance and the living conditions that it provides for the parrot will be dramatically improved.

There are no secrets in caring for the parrot so that it will lead a healthy life. Common everyday judgment, attention paid to its diet and grooming needs, and understanding and love are all that are needed for a pet which can provide years of companionship and pleasure.

Chapter 9
Taming Your Larger Parrot

Since most parrots are still basically wild when they are purchased, a pet owner is faced with what can sometimes appear to be a formidable task in trying to tame his new pet—to civilize it to the ways of man, so to speak. Whether this new bird is a tiny critter like a budgie or a monster-sized macaw, the bird has rarely left its pet store cage voluntarily and in good spirits. It almost always had to be physically hauled from its cage, during which time it screamed, flared out its wings, slashed with its beak, held on to its cage for dear life, and in every way presented itself as the antithesis of the charming pet parrot always encountered in zoos and circuses.

With the larger parrots, the salesman may have had to protect himself with heavy welding gloves when evicting the bird from its cage and more often than not received several bites in the process.

Such struggles between beast and man must invariably raise serious doubts in the master's mind. Is a parrot really necessary? Wouldn't a cute little puppy do just as well as a pet for the kids? And always, I would venture to guess, there is that haunting doubt as to whether we are really quite up to the task of taming that feathered demon.

These kinds of doubts are normal. Indeed, if anything, they make us acutely aware of the bird's psychological condition which is a prerequisite if we are to adequately cope with our own feelings and the task of taming the bird. The parrot's behavior is a result of its fear of man, nothing more. If it were not afraid of man—terrorized would probably be a more appropriate word—it would seize the opportunity to beg for food and head scratching. But as discussed earlier in the book, the parrot has good reason to fear man. And that fear of man includes the present owner.

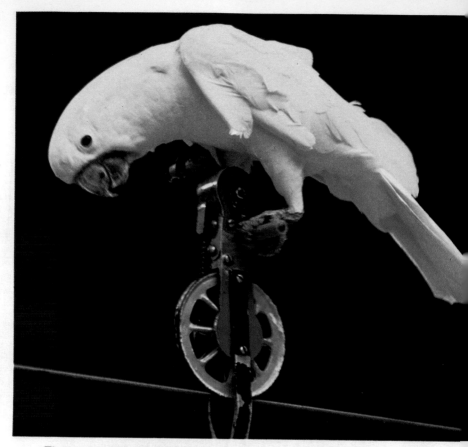

The complexity of the tricks that a parrot will learn is limited only by the trainer's imagination and the natural ability of the bird, given its physical limitations. Riding a bicycle is a difficult feat, but riding a unicycle on a tightrope is an extraordinary feat; yet it is one which proves that even such complex maneuvers are not beyond the physical limitations of some parrots. This is a Blue Eyed Cockatoo (*Cacatua ophthalmica*).

Opposite:
A Moluccan Cockatoo which accepts human love and friendship is a delightful animal which will have no limits to the kinds of handling it will accept. This gentle bird, called Babsy, tamed by the author and held by Donna Rosinko, is owned by Richard Favorite.

220

There is an irony to this matter of fear, for while the parrot is deadly afraid of contact with man, the parrot owner is usually more afraid of the parrot. Even though parrots do not kill people. Even though parrots do not mishandle man. Even though parrots have not deprived man of his freedom.

Regardless of how much fear the owner may have for his new exotic bird, the truth is that the parrot will never truly inflict much serious pain or injury on its owner. It is sometimes difficult to convince people of that fact. As a case of point, some years ago we ran advertisements in local newspapers advertising our services in taming and training parrots. Most of the bird owners who brought parrots to us for taming were generally bird fanciers who had just acquired a particular bird or another but lacked sufficient skill (or courage) in taming their pet; sometimes a parrot was delivered to our doorstep which had been in the family for months, even years, and which was totally incorrigible and indeed a poor prospect for remedial training.

It is natural to be apprehensive about taming what is normally only a handful of feathers—a handful, however, which takes on demonic features when it is approached for that final confrontation between man and beast. But regardless of how apprehensive or frightened the owner may be, it is the bird whose fear is greater. After all, it has lost every battle in its encounters with man, just as it will lose this one. It is faced with a creature many times its size and strength—a creature which, from all of its previous experience, promises to again inflict hardship and pain.

It is therefore extremely important to remember just who is more afraid of whom. When a bird tamer is more afraid of the bird than it is of him, then all training sessions will be contaminated by that fear, and the trainer who allows himself to become intimidated by the parrot automatically concedes control of the training to the bird. Instead of man mastering the beast, it is beast which masters the man.

This is not to suggest that the trainer should forge ahead in his task without a healthy respect for the bird's ability to bite—and sometimes bite hard. Even a little bird can inflict a painful bite if its tiny beak grabs a hapless cuticle. Caution is necessary, particularly with the larger exotics during the preliminary training sessions, but caution should never be governed by fear.

222

All birds, regardless of how ferocious they may seem when approached at close quarters, would rather flee than face a combat with man. When flight is impossible, a terrorized bird may attempt to intimidate the trainer. With flared wings, hissing, shreiking, raised crest, dancing behavior, and lunges which are supposed to keep the trainer at bay, the parrot attempts to frighten away its adversary.

If flight or intimidation fail, the terrorized parrot may attempt to bury its head in a corner or beneath a newspaper or what have you—as if to make itself so small that the person will not notice it. But this attempt at hiding is nothing more than a normal fear reaction, no different from a normal human response should a dinosaur come rampaging down the street towards us.

Whatever the bird's response to the trainer, it is a rare bird which actually attempts to attack the person. Since the parrot is afraid, it becomes the owner's main objective to show the bird that there is nothing to fear from man and that men are capable and willing to be kind and loving.

Given this understanding, and before we actually begin our task of taming the parrot, a word or two about the philosophy of taming is in order. It is unfortunate, but true, that some trainers use extremely barbaric methods to tame their birds. One bird trainer in southern California offers workshops in bird training in which he advocates hitting the bird across the beak when it attempts to bite, squirting it with water, pulling its tail. Such tactics do work, I am sure, but at what price?

Many so called "bird lovers" perpetuate another form of cruelty and barbarism to their pet birds. They attach a lengthy cord or chain to the parrot's leg and secure the other end on a hand if out in the open or on some stable fixture if indoors. The practice is particularly barbaric because frequently, should the bird become frightened, it attempts to fly away, becomes entangled in the fetter, and in its struggles often seriously injures itself, frequently breaking a wing or leg.

If the bird is not tame enough to trust, then the master should not take it outside without first trimming its primaries. Too often, however, the master is so vain that he delights in flaunting the parrot to others at the risk of injuring the bird.

The parrot fears man. It has had ugly experiences with man, and

Certain kinds of tricks are unsuitable for some parrots. Roller skating is a trick best taught to macaws in preference to other species. Part of the reason lies in the size of the skates and part in the shape, size and balance of the bird.

Opposite:
Margo Robinson is very fortunate indeed to have Damion as a pet. This Military Macaw *(Ara militaris)* likes to quarrel with Margo when she wants him to do something that does not particularly appeal to him at the moment. His raucous protests are nothing more than that, for he wouldn't harm a soul. This bird's behavior conveys the impression that anyone could do virtually any thing he wanted with this beautiful and gentle creature without fear of being bitten.

it therefore has no reason to trust him, let alone willingly accept him into its life. Inflicting further hurt and terror onto the bird seems scarcely a technique to win confidence, love, and trust. A parrot which is tamed in this manner is not a pet which comes willingly to its master, which willingly seeks comfort and companionship, which willingly offers itself into a relationship. It is a bird tamed by fear, responding to fear, governed by fear.

Compassion, understanding, and love govern our method of training birds, even when we have suffered the most painful of bites. If we cannot win a parrot's confidence and trust with this approach, then the parrot is not the kind of bird we would want for a pet—a parrot whose submission through force makes it an unwilling partner between master and animal. If the parrot cannot be won over by love, it is best to sell it, even at a loss, and buy another parrot. The loss is well worth the gain that accrues from a parrot with a more adaptable disposition which is friendly, warm, and loving.

GETTING READY FOR THE FIRST ENCOUNTER

Taming a wild parrot is the process of molding the bird into certain specific patterns of behavior so that master and pet can interact in a harmonious fashion. Therefore, in order for a wild parrot to become transformed into a tame pet, it must be taught to accept being touched, to accept being picked up, to accept being held close, and to accept its master(s) enough so that it will get on a hand when the hand is offered it. Most birds can learn to relate to man in intimate ways, more or less depending on the species.

a) Being touched: The parrot is taught that when it is touched no harm will come to it. In the process of learning that there is no danger, the bird also learns that there is no need to bite. This does not imply, however, that a parrot which accepts the human touch will never bite someone. The parrot may not feel well, it may have been teased or molested, and consequently may at some time bite its owner. But once it begins learning that no harm will come from the human hand, the frequency of bites will diminish accordingly and eventually become for all practical purposes non-existent.

b) Being picked up: The parrot is taught that no harm will come to it should it be physically picked up by one or both hands. The

226

matter referred to here is the act of picking up the bird in the same manner as one would a cat or dog. Smaller birds learn to be picked up with one hand holding them about the middle. Teaching a bird to be picked up in this fashion has several important consequences: the parrot learns to trust the person handling it; it is easier then to teach the bird to be cuddled; and the parrot is easier to handle during the initial stages of taming and later when, because it has been frightened for one reason or another, it refuses to step onto a hand on command.

Unfortunately, many bird trainers bypass this important aspect of training. While this step in the parrot's training is not essential to its tameness or its quality as a pet, it does nevertheless better prepare the parrot for later acceptance of intimate handling.

c) Being held close: The parrot is taught that no harm will come to it when it is cuddled, held close to the body, cupped in one's hands, or otherwise physically held/constrained to the master's body. A parrot which learns to trust close physical proximity to its master is a bird more prone to seek affection. It is a bird which will prefer to be with or on its master rather than be apart. Our Selsa, as an example, is a parrot who loves to be cradled in our arms while lying on her back.

Unfortunately, too, many trainers ignore this important aspect of the parrot's socialization. The parrot will not automatically become affectionate and gregarious. By ignoring this important aspect of training, valuable time is sacrificed in fully incorporating the parrot into family life.

d) Stepping on the hand: This aspect of the parrot's taming centers on teaching the bird to get on the hand on command. By *on command* we mean that a finger or hand when presented to the bird is an automatic instruction for the bird to stop doing whatever it is doing and to get on. It means that the parrot will get on the hand regardless of whether it is expected to walk from one hand to another, from the floor to the hand, from the top of the cage to the hand, from the interior of the cage to the hand, or any other place where it may be perched to the hand.

Frequently, trainers tame their parrots to get on the hand should the bird be on the floor or to walk from hand to hand, but as soon as the parrot is inside its cage, it refuses to step onto the hand that is offered it. Such a bird is inadequately trained—namely, the bird

A parrot which can perform complex tricks such as the one above is evidence of a good working relationship between man and beast. It is also indicative of the love and care which a master devotes to the parrot. The attachment between the bird and person becomes intense as a result of training.

Opposite:
This Sulphur Crested Cockatoo *(Cacatua galerita galerita)* is a beautiful creature which performs regularly at the Busch Bird Sanctuary in California. It is one of the subspecies which is often referred to in the United States as the Greater Sulphur Crested Cockatoo. Indeed, it is the largest of all the ten recognized Lesser Sulphur and Sulphur Crested Cockatoos.

refuses to leave the comfort of its cage for the uncertainties of the hand. Further training is required and that training requires basically nothing more than some repetitious exercises.

Parrots can be classified into two basic types of tamability. There are those which because of age, species, abuse by man, and a variety of more subtle causes are birds whose tameness is basically nothing more than a bare tolerance of the master. It is a bird which will in most probability get on a hand on command, which will not bite people with any frequent occurrence, but which will be for the most part unapproachable. It will be a parrot attractive in appearance which might talk but which will remain aloof from intimate contact with humans.

Then there are those tamed exotic birds which crave relationships with their masters. They are birds which cry out in excitement when their master arrives home. Their happiest moments are when they are perched on the master's shoulder or when they are having their head scratched. If the master moves to another room in the house, the bird follows him like a puppy. From our experience, the basic ingredient essential to taming a parrot so that it becomes an affectionate and gregarious pet instead of a bird which barely tolerates people—given that all factors are equal—is the amount of time a master is prepared to devote to his pet. We encourage the bird lover to allow their pets freedom within the home environment; we particularly recommend that they perform some of their housework during the day with the parrot on the shoulder, such as when washing the dishes or vacuuming the house. This extra time spent daily with the bird strengthens the bond between bird and master and concurrently discourages the tendency to independent behavior that is part of the bird's instinctual patterns, regardless of whether the bird is small or large.

For the purpose of our discussion in this chapter, parrots and parrot types can also be arbitrarily grouped into large birds, medium sized birds, and small birds. While there are many methods of taming birds, the method which is being recommended here is the simplest and most uncomplicated way for the average bird fancier to achieve quick and permanent results. In loosely classifying birds into three distinct groups, slightly different taming methods will be employed with each. The strategy for all remains the same, however.

Our grouping of large birds will include all macaws and all large cockatoos, including the Lesser Sulphur. (Most cockatoos are included because of the type of bite they can inflict—a point which will be discussed shortly.) The medium sized parrot would include birds the size of the Red Head, Mealy Amazon, Blue Fronted Amazon, African Grey, and so on. Smaller birds can be defined as those the size of conures, cockatiels, beebee parrots, lovebirds, and those of similar size. Since the classifications are arbitrary and subject to judgment, a parrot can easily be reclassified without harm if the method of taming in one classification seems inappropriate to it after a working session or two.

TAMING THE LARGE PARROT

While the smaller birds can deliver a bite which not only smarts but which may draw blood, it is the larger exotic birds which have the capacity to severely lacerate a finger. It is often said, for example, that the larger Macaws can exert up to 900 pounds pressure per square inch. Moreover, some types of birds, the cockatoos for example, have beaks which can inflict far more injury than the beaks of other bird types. Because cockatoos grind their mandibles together in order to reduce beak growth, the lower mandible has two sharp points to it. When a cockatoo grabs the fleshy part of a finger or wrist, not only does the upper mandible point penetrate into the flesh, but the lower mandible with its two points punctures the skin in two places. Should a trainer be unfortunately seized by such a beak, he will soon find that not only does the cockatoo hold tenaciously to its victim, but that the three punctures will seem to drip a copious amount of blood. It is not very much fun trying to pry such a beak open with the free hand while watching one's life juices drip away to stain the carpet, this at a time when the pain seems excruciating. In such cases, the trainer must endure the pain, pry open the offending beak, and rush into the bathroom before screaming and cursing. A dutiful spouse skilled in first aid is always helpful on such occasions.

Thus, because of their size and the kind of bites some parrots can inflict, 'larger birds' are more difficult to handle. To adequately prepare oneself for the taming sessions with such birds, the trainer will need a pair of heavy duty welding gloves, a stand-

Practical considerations have to be taken into account when one is deciding the kinds of tricks to teach the bird to perform. Certain tricks and stunts are more appropriate for circuses than for home entertainment. Riding a bicycle is a clever trick for a parrot, but tricks like playing dead, picking up and answering a telephone when it rings, coming when called and others, for example, are less costly in terms of equipment and time required for training—and they're just as effective in developing a strong bond between owner and bird and in providing a source of amusement for friends.

This Medium Sulphur Crested Cockatoo *(Cacatua galerita)* is the prized pet of Sandra Platt of Long Beach, California.

ing perch, a quiet room in the home, and an enclosed area within that room. The parrot should be prepared before handling by trimming its talons and clipping its wings.

The heavy duty gloves are essential for, while they do not prevent the parrot from inflicting some pain should the trainer be careless enough to get bitten, they are an excellent safeguard against lacerations. With some parrots, such as Moluccan Cockatoos, I use two pairs of gloves: a heavy duty rubber glove as used in washing automobiles over which is worn a heavy pair of welding gloves.

The standing perch is an important item during the last stage of training the parrot. With scraps of lumber, a perch can be made within a few minutes. A three-foot pipe or two-by-two is attached to a twelve-inch board base. A two-inch diameter dowel or tree branch is then attached to the stand. While this type of perch is preferable, a simple chair with a wooden arm rest or a card table chair will do just as well.

Finally, the best room in which to work the bird is where there are no distractions and noises, a room where the bird only has to contend with one person to which it gives all its attention, at least during the first part of the taming. A parrot which feels threatened from all quarters by numerous persons or things is a bird which cannot focus its attention on the tasks ahead of it because of this increased terror.

Further, the room should have some type of narrow enclosure in it which will restrict the bird's movements. Most bathrooms are ideal. In our dressing area adjacent to the bathroom we have a vanity under which we keep a weighing scale and a small waste paper basket. It is an area approximately three feet long by two feet high by eighteen inches deep. With the basket and weigh scale removed, the enclosure is ideal because when placed within it, the parrot has nowhere to flee at a time when its sole interest is escape. The vanity top provides no upward escape route, and when I am seated in front of the parrot, it has no opportunity to escape on either my right or left hand sides because both routes can be easily blocked by a hand. Few parrots will try to climb over their trainers, but some of the more ingenious and courageous parrots have been known to do so from time to time. Lacking the type of alcove mentioned above, a corner of the room will suffice, although it is somewhat more restricted in size.

As noted earlier, it is always best to do the taming and training in another room away from the one containing the cage. Because the parrot perceives its cage as its private sanctuary, and its immediate goal is to return to the cage when it is being harassed, it will be difficult to maintain the parrot's interest during the training session as long as cage and bird are in the same room.

The object of restricting the training area to such a small enclosure is to prevent the bird from fleeing. The more often the parrot escapes from its master, the more often the terrorized bird must be chased about the room in order to catch it. Of course, the greater the terror of the bird as a result of the chasing and capture, the greater the stress.

Once a suitable training area has been located, remove the parrot from the cage. The task may seem more difficult than it is. At the first opportunity which presents itself, grab the wild bird behind the head with the forefinger closing up firmly, but not tightly, against the lower mandible to prevent the beak from reaching around to bite. With the other hand pin the bird's flapping wings to its body to prevent further struggles during which it could injure itself. After removing the parrot from the cage, release it in the corner chosen for the initial taming session.

Another way of removing the parrot from the cage is by grabbing onto the parrot's leg and holding on. The bird will immediately resist withdrawal by seizing hold of the cage bars or perch with beak and free foot. Eventually, however, the parrot will tire and will relinquish its hold so that it can be removed from the cage. The parrot should never be seized by the wing because the wing is extremely fragile and there is an acute danger of possibly breaking it.

Taking the parrot to the selected training area, close the door, sit before the enclosure, and release the bird into it. The parrot's first reaction is normally one of panic so that it will attempt to flee. Prevent escape by blocking off the escape routes with either the hands or body. There is no need to abuse the bird; if it escapes, it escapes. Should the parrot outwit the blockades, recapture it, securing it as noted earlier, and return it to the enclosure. Within a very short time, the parrot will realize that it cannot escape. Moreover, at that time it also usually learns that nothing drastic

After your parrot is accustomed to being handled and carried, it is time to teach it to step on your hand whenever your hand is presented to the bird. You might want to put your glove back on when you begin this training, as the bird might bite you—not so much out of fear but because it might use its beak as a hand to help regain its balance after the move.

Opposite:
The colorful Scarlet Macaw *(Ara macao)* is readily recognized by the predominance of red over the upper part of its body and on the tail. It is a rare Scarlet which does not prove to be a gentle, sensitive pet, and it sometimes is known to talk. While their calls are harsh, captive pet Scarlets are not too noisy. As with all intelligent parrots, the Scarlets should be given ample wooden materials to gnaw and play with. Good emotional health is ensured by an environment which permits ample activity.

will happen to it because it is in the enclosure, and the panic will therefore subside. But the battle is still far from won.

Once the fleeing tactics have ended, the parrot may either try to attack the tamer's hands or else try to hide itself by burying its head in the corner. Should the parrot attack—which only infrequently happens—the attack will always be focused on the hand because it is what the bird associates with all its unpleasant encounters with man. The attacks can easily be repulsed by balling the hand into a fist and presenting the back of the fist to the parrot's beak. The parrot will soon learn that it cannot seize hold of any part of a fist, and the attacks will cease.

Should the parrot cower with its head in the corner, gently but cautiously force a hand between bird and wall and push the bird away from the corner.

Another tactic that the parrot may use is a remarkably realistic and successful method which intimidates quite a few first-time parrot trainers: the parrot screams incessantly, flares out its wings, struts back and forth menacingly, and presents itself as a ferocious beast.

There is no need to back down from the parrot, however, for there is no damage the parrot can really do. He is all bluff.

During all these various types of maneuvers and all subsequent activities related to the training sessions, *the trainer should always remain calm, and his movements should always be slow enough so that they are not interpreted as threats by the fear-ridden bird. The trainer should also speak in a soft and low monotone, a monotone which is continuous without pause.*

The purpose of the monotone is two-fold: it serves as a vehicle for calming the parrot and also as the means by which the parrot must eventually learn the meaning of the word "NO."

Once the parrot shows signs of quieting, the actual training can begin. With considerable caution, touch the parrot's wing with one hand. The parrot will try to bite the hand and so the first few attempts to touch a wing may prove to be unsuccessful because the bird may be swifter at protecting its flank than the trainer is at touching the wing. Eventually, however, after a few attempts, it will be possible to touch the wing because the parrot begins to both tire and to become less concerned about the hand being a threat to it.

238

A good tactic to try is touching one wing and then the other, thereby keeping the parrot's defenses 'off balance.'

During these wing touching exercises, eyes should never be taken off the bird for it can react very swiftly in seizing a hapless finger in its terror and defense. Indeed, most injuries occur because the trainer's mind has wandered.

By touching the bird's wing with one hand and the other wing with the other hand, maintaining a steady and constant pace, repeating this activity until the parrot stops trying to bite the hand, the trainer will soon notice that the bird's reaction to the hand's touch will begin to dramatically slow down. Eventually, the parrot will make motions, feints, at grabbing the hand but they will fall short of seizing it. The feints are an attempt by the bird in maintaining its bluff posture.

Once the speed and the intent of a potential bite have become less threatening, that is the clue for the trainer to let his hand linger on each wing. The length of time which a finger or hand can linger will be determined by the parrot's increasing tolerance of accepting what it once perceived as a direct threat to it.

When it becomes evident that the parrot will accept its wings being touched, it is time for the trainer to begin focusing his attention on the parrot's breast and feet. Continue stroking the wings, but on every second or third stroke touch the breast or foot instead. Because the hand will now be more vulnerable and easier to attack, the trainer should be extremely cautious. As acceptance of breast and foot touching begins increasing, less attention should be given to the wings in preference to the breast and feet. Again, as before, both hands should be used to keep the parrot's defenses off balance.

Some judgment should be exercised at this point. Some parrots cannot be worked any more than five or ten minutes while others may be worked hard for half an hour or so. Some parrots will accept wing, breast, and even foot touching after the end of a fifteen-minute lesson while other parrots will not even accept wing touching after the first half hour lesson. *Judgment is necessary so that the lesson will end before the parrot's tolerance level has been surpassed and an excessive stress level reached.*

As a general rule, most parrots will permit lingering wing touches within the first ten to fifteen minutes of their first lesson,

The beautiful Sulphur Crested Cockatoo *(Cacatua galerita galerita)*, either frightened or simply showing off (as many like to do), is a perennial favorite. While Australia no longer exports them, enough numbers are being bred in captivity so that pet fanciers are occasionally able to purchase them through pet shops or breeders. One of four races common to the Sulphur Crested Cockatoo, the individual shown here is sometimes mistakenly called a 'Greater' Sulphur Crested Cockatoo because it is larger than the other three races; it is then mistakenly treated as a separate species of cockatoo—it is actually only a subspecies. The 'Greater' Sulphur Crested Cockatoo is a desirable parrot which commands a high premium.

Opposite:
The Red Bellied Macaw *(Ara manilata)* is commonly found throughout northern South America. Because of its size, it is sometimes referred to as belonging to the 'miniature' macaws, a group of macaws which are not as desirable as pets as are the larger macaws (such as the Blue and Gold, Hyacinth, Scarlet or Military). The Red Bellied is infrequently encountered in the pet trade.

and some will even accept breast and feet contact. During the first lesson, we rarely work the parrot beyond twenty minutes, regardless of what progress it has made or failed to make. We prefer to play it safe.

If progress is made and the parrot accepts wing stroking without becoming alarmed, that does not mean the parrot has given his trainer his permission because it enjoys being touched. It does mean, however, that the bird is no longer thoroughly terrorized when faced with a human hand! Given its previous experience with humans, such a permission is a remarkable step forward on the part of the parrot. The trainer should feel pleased.

After its first taming lesson, return the parrot to its cage. Almost invariably, the bird will have to be returned to the cage much in the manner in which it was removed from it. But since the parrot is unconfined, less force will be required to capture it and therefore the experience will be less traumatic for the bird. Once the parrot is returned to the cage, if possible and with caution, offer it some tidbit that it prefers. It may very well accept it.

Between working sessions, position the cage where there is substantial traffic in the home, such as in the kitchen. Whenever approaching the cage, approach it slowly, always speaking in a quiet monotone to the parrot. *Always be deliberate and quiet in manner and voice. Avoid appearing like a threat.*

If the parrot calms down satisfactorily when returned to the cage—this can easily be determined by noting whether the bird resumes its normal habits, particularly eating—give the parrot its next working session four or five hours later in exactly the same manner as prescribed above. The second training session should begin with wing touching exercises, regardless of the parrot's progress at the end of the first confrontation. Should the bird resume its earlier pattern of flight or attack behavior, the trainer will soon note that such behavior will be short-lived. As soon as the parrot accepts the wing touching, attention should resume where it left off with the previous lesson.

By proceeding from wings to breast and feet, and then to other parts of the body, the parrot will eventually learn to accept the human touch without becoming unduly alarmed. The head is probably the last place that the exercises should focus on because many birds resent head touching and will accept it only when they thoroughly trust the trainer. Should the parrot show no inordinate amount of fear at having its head touched, try scratching its nape. Another good trick to remember, once a parrot begins accepting wing and breast touching, is to gently slide a forefinger under the bird's wing and caress the body. After one or two such attempts the trainer will be delightfully surprised to see the wing lift up to welcome the finger.

That is always a good sign because the trainer can now assume that a major part of the battle has been won: the parrot is now beginning to associate the hand with pleasure, instead of hurt.

During the second working session, depending on the progress of the bird, we normally try to teach it the meaning of "No." We have emphasized the importance of the quiet monotone in calming the parrot. The parrot, showing progress, is by no means tamed and is still inclined to bite. Once the parrot has become accustomed to the monotone and, during the course of the second or third lesson tries to bite or does bite, the monotone should be broken with a sharp and loud "NO." This dramatic break from the monotone almost always startles the bird and it will stop whatever it is doing to look at the source of its discomfort.

Every time the parrot attempts to bite, this loud and sharp "No" should be yelled at the bird. This technique, incidently, is useless with a parrot which is totally wild or which has not yet showed signs of taming. With each "No," the parrot will generally react by ceasing its offending behavior, provided of course the monotone had been used long enough to have become an important aspect in the bird's training. Once the parrot begins normally reacting to the word "no," it will no longer have to be yelled out; the parrot will recognize the sound when it is used in a monotone, the normal training voice. The parrot will soon transfer the admonition to other behaviors so that later, when the parrot is involved in some mischief, a "no" command will generally stop the bird from carrying on, at least temporarily.

As noted earlier, each bird will progress at its own rate according to its own abilities and tolerance level. At some point the trainer will observe that the bird will accept a human's touch almost anywhere on the body without becoming terrorized. At that point, the gloves should be removed.

Although the parrot is accustomed to a gloved hand, a bare hand

Even a Green Winged Macaw *(Ara chloroptera)* from South America can be taught to be patriotic.

Opposite:
While not as colorful in appearance as the other macaws, the Military Macaw can be easily trained to perform tricks and can prove to be a gentle and affectionate pet. This young bird, Damion, will virtually turn over on his back every time a hand will provide him the support. While in this awkward position Damion will lie still for minutes on end. Damion is owned by Norma Robinson of Newport Beach, California.

245

often becomes a totally different issue when viewed from the bird's perspective. As soon as the bare hand touches the parrot, the trainer may be unpleasantly shocked to find that not only have the ferocity of attacks resumed, but that he has been bitten. Until secure in the knowledge that the parrot will not bite a bare hand, just as it had learned not to bite the gloved hand, then the trainer must exercise caution.

Should the bird resist being touched with a bare hand, renew the touching exercises as before when using a gloved hand: wings first, then breast, feet, back, head. At the beginning, however, the trainer's touch may have to be swift and secure until the bird realizes that there is no more harm in the bare hand than there was in a gloved hand. The parrot's initial fear of a bare hand can usually be conquered within a few minutes.

Scratching a bird's head, caressing its wing pits, and gently patting it on the back are always touches which are enjoyed by the parrot. We also like to give our parrots a break every few minutes during which the parrot is offered a tidbit which it has shown a preference for.

Once the parrot can be handled without fear of having a bare hand bitten, the bird is ready to develop a stronger trust relationship with its master. At this point we begin the second stage of the parrot's taming, the stage in which the parrot learns to be picked up as one would a kitten.

To teach the parrot to accept two hands enclosing it, it may again be necessary to protect the hands with gloves. If the bird does bite, it will no longer bite out of fear. Rather, the parrot will unintentionally bite the trainer because when the parrot is lifted bodily, it senses its loss of weight and control over itself and may seize a finger in its attempt to regain its balance.

Return the parrot to the enclosed training area—an area in which it should now feel comfortable. Gently wrapping both hands around the lower portion of the parrot, put an upward pressure on the bird as if in lifting it up, pinning both wings to its body gently but firmly, but do not completely lift the bird from the floor. Release the bird and repeat the exercise several times, always being sure that sufficient upward pressure is put on the parrot so that it can sense its slight loss of balance and the upward pressure of the hand.

246

The parrot will soon become accustomed to this sensation and will accept the encompassing hands and the slight upward motion.

As soon as the parrot shows acceptance, lift the parrot an inch or so from the floor and immediately release it again. Repeat this process of clearing the bird from the floor several times, each time lifting it an inch or so higher than before. Most large parrots will learn to accept this aspect of their training within six to eight minutes.

In this exercise, it is important that the parrot be firmly clasped about the wings so that it cannot struggle. If the parrot's wings are not held closely, it may eventually free one of them, thereby increasing its sensation of loss of balance and hence making the whole exercise futile. A comfortable but firm hold helps develop trust.

Once the parrot accepts itself being picked up off the floor, pick it up and bodily carry it to another part of the room where it should be immediately released. The parrot should thereafter be picked up several times and each time carried to a different part of the building. Should the bird begin to struggle violently, immediately release the bird, wait a second or two until its panic subsides, and resume the exercise.

The parrot's confidence in this type of handling will soon be evidenced when *the parrot stops still and waits to be picked up as soon as it notices the two hands coming towards it.* Our experience has been that most larger parrots will learn to accept this kind of handling very easily within ten minutes. While there are distinct advantages to picking up a parrot with either one or both hands encompassing it, the method should be used sparingly once the parrot has been taught to accept this method of handling. Moisture from the hands and the friction between feathers and hands can ruin a parrot's feathered appearance if overused. The feathers have natural oils or powders which provide the plumage with both protection and sheen. Overhandling can deleteriously affect the bird's wardrobe regardless of how much the parrot may groom itself.

The third stage of the parrot's taming involves teaching it to accept being held close to the trainer's body. While the bird may now seem willing to accept such intimacy, should we try to cuddle the bird while holding it with two hands we may find that the bird

Most of the larger parrots, such as this Blue and Gold Macaw *(Ara ararauna)*, exhibit a great deal of sensitivity to and interest in their environment. They enjoy exploring novel situations and can often get into quite a bit of mischief if given the opportunity. One solution which some pet owners have taken, unfortunately, is to keep these intelligent creatures locked in confined quarters with limited opportunity to exercise their imaginations. A far better solution, once the bird is tamed, is to give it reasonable freedom in its particular environment and to provide it with ample toys, usually hard wooden pieces which it can chew and manipulate at its heart's content. Because they will destroy wooden toys within days, there is always the problem of replacing them, but that is a small price to pay for having a contented and emotionally fit pet.

Opposite:
Steve Herried of Huntington Beach has an excellent relationship with his Sulphur Crested Cockatoo, Cuervo. Cuevro will accept all kinds of handling, and he seems to enjoy every minute with his master. Cuervo, however, just hates to have his feet touched. Usually a quiet bird, he lets out a squawk of protest and flares his crest whenever anyone dares to touch his foot. One of the things Cuervo really enjoys is having his master whisper in his ear.

249

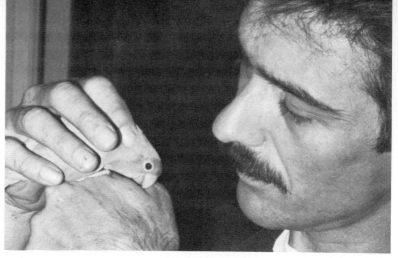

As much as it may seem unnatural to the reader, birds will accept close handling as seen in this picture. Indeed, scratch its nape and crown and the bird will accept such confines with pleasure for hours on end.

will react as if claustrophobic. It will struggle and perhaps even bite in its fear. To overcome this claustrophobia, we use deceptive strategy in training the parrot to accept intimacy.

We introduce the parrot to increasing degrees of closeness every time we pick the bird up and transport it to another part of the house. Since the parrot normally shows more interest in where it is going than what is happening to it, we use the occasion of transporting to hold the bird just that much closer with each successive trip. By cheating this way, we are able to deceive the parrot enough so that it never really has a chance to become claustrophobic because before it really knows what has happened, it has become conditioned to close proximity. Most birds will accept this close proximity within short order. Many will even accept being carried under the arm or in the crook of the arm within two or three minutes!

Now that the parrot can be picked up at will and held close to the body, it is an appropriate time to scratch its head or nape. Giving it treats is also a good tactic. The parrot soon learns that being held close to the master is not only pleasurable, but that it also provides dividends.

Our final stage in taming the bird is to train it to get onto the hand on command. To remind the reader: to *get on the hand on command* means that the extended hand is a cue to which the parrot responds by automatically stepping onto it. This means that the parrot will step onto the hand regardless of where it may be at that moment—unless for some reason the bird has been severely frightened by something, a reaction which anyone can understand.

Our objective at this point is to develop the bird's reflexes to such an extent that it will step onto the hand as automatically as our foot slams on the brake should a child dart in front of our traveling vehicle.

Many manuals instructing owners in parrot training recommend the 'stick method' of teaching their bird to step onto a hand. Instead of presenting a parrot with a hand during this stage of its training, the trainer uses a stick onto which the bird is supposed to step. Regrettably, many parrots never go beyond the 'stick stage' of their training. It has always seemed incongruous to this writer that bird owners boast of their so-called tamed pet when that bird will never leave its cage without a struggle unless a stick has been first shoved into its abode!

Succinctly, the stick method has very little value since the parrot already knows how to step onto a branch. Using this method needlessly harasses the bird and unnecessarily frustrates the trainer. It is the hand which is the obstacle and which must be mastered by the bird. Not the stick!

Furthermore, training the bird with a stick is a time-consuming method. First the bird must learn to step onto the stick, and then the trainer must somehow get the parrot to transfer that new learning to stepping onto his hand.

We just forget about stick training and get right to the problem from the beginning.

The hand is large and complex, unlike the cylindrical shape of all branches and sticks. The parrot must learn how to best grab onto the hand which is offered it. For a parrot, that can be a problem during the first few attempts.

To train a parrot to mount the hand on command, first return to the training room. Place the perch, or its facsimile, in the middle of the room with a chair facing it. After seating yourself in the chair, place the parrot on the perch.

251

The Galah *(Eolophus roseicapillus)*, sometimes called the Rose Breasted Cockatoo, is one of the loveliest of Australian birds. Unfortunately, it is seldom encountered outside of its homeland.

Opposite:
The Palm Cockatoo *Probosciger aterrimus goliath*, is a large bird, about thirty inches in length. Its grayish black coloring and its red facial patch give it a rather mean appearance, but it is actually affectionate and gentle. Palm Cockatoos inhabit Australia and are not often seen as pets in this country.

Extend the back of the hand to the parrot and push against the bird at the point where body and thighs meet. Push the parrot backwards as if to topple it from the perch, so that when losing balance it will step onto the hand in order to regain equilibrium. This is the theory. But, more often than not, the bird will either try to sidestep the pushy hand, jump off the perch, or attempt to climb down.

Should the parrot try sidestepping, put your hand in front of it again and push once more. Should it jump to the floor, immediately pick it up and return it to the perch. If the parrot attempts to climb down, put a hand under it and gently force it back onto the perch.

Under no circumstances should the trainer allow the parrot to escape its lesson. Be persistent, otherwise it will all be to no avail.

Eventually, a great many parrots will just balk, yes balk, at the exercise. They will just refuse to do anything and everything. After all, what respectable parrot wants to be pushed off a comfortable perch by some unreasonable clod who thinks he is some kind of lion tamer?

Such parrots have a tendency to believe they are immovable, something akin to a Rock of Gibraltar. The trainer should not be deceived, however. If when pushed the parrot refuses to get on the hand, then, using the other hand, push the bird forward. Caught between two pushes, the poor devil almost always takes the path of least resistance and steps forward.

The first few attempts to climb onto the hand will usually be accompanied by considerable beak assistance. For the exceptionally large birds, it is best to use gloves until the parrot shows signs of mastering the awkwardness of having to step onto a cumbersome hand. Soon the bird will learn to get onto the hand without first relying on its beak for support, at least most of the time. As the bird begins to show mastery, the glove can be discarded.

It should be pointed out that the parrot uses its beak solely as a means of climbing; it is not being used as a weapon. The glove is only used in the possibility that the parrot may inadvertently grab a finger or wrist with too much pressure during its first few attempts to clamber onto the hand.

Once the parrot begins stepping onto the hand regularly, even though it may still have to be pushed from time to time when its interest flags, increase the pace of the exercise until it is stepping on and off the hand at a tempo of several times a minute. By the end of its first session, it should be getting on and off every five or six seconds. Of course, there should be frequent, but brief, rest stops. In all, that first on-off work session should last between twenty and thirty minutes.

Once the parrot steps onto the hand gracefully and confidently and no longer needs its beak to maintain equilibrium, put the bird on top of its cage to see if it will respond as it did a few seconds earlier. The probability is that it will refuse to obey the hand command—something it seemed to do so naturally just a minute or so before.

Remember that it is normal for the parrot to balk at hand perching once it is sitting on a cage, which is synonymous with safety. The trainer has been submitting the parrot to uncertainty, conflict, and an alien situation. A cage, on the other hand, even for the wildest of birds, represents in the parrot's eye its only sanctuary from the threats and indignities which are its lot whenever it is in the company of man. No sane parrot, uncertain with the 'pie in the sky' promises of an extended hand, will voluntarily leave its cage unless thoroughly conditioned to do so.

After a three- or four-hour rest period, resume the training on the perch. The lesson should persist half an hour or so. This time, however, there will be little resistance on the parrot's part. The more automatic and perfected the stepping on-off behavior, the greater the probability that the bird will be enticed off its cage and later off its perch in the cage when you present your hand.

Return the parrot to the cage top and test it again. Should the bird momentarily balk, push it forward onto the extended hand. Continue pushing it every time it balks until the bird begins stepping on automatically. Most birds, by this stage of their conditioning, will step onto a hand within a minute or two—after the first gentle push—when they learn that there is really no respite from a persistent person.

Finally, return the bird back to the cage and let it get onto its perch. This is the supreme test of your lion taming skills. Extend the hand and test the bird as when it was on the top of its cage and on its work perch. The bird will most probably get on and allow you to remove it from the cage.

The Gang Gang Cockatoo *(Callocephalon fimbriatum)* is a rather plain looking cockatoo which inhabits the extreme southeastern region of Australia. It appears to be diminishing in numbers,

The Little Corella *(Cacatua sanguinea)* is an Australian species which occupies a significantly large part of Australia's land mass. While the species breeds in captivity, it is rarely encountered in the United States. This is probably due to the fact that when exotic birds were still freely imported from Australia, this species was generally overlooked in favor of the wide variety of more colorful and intelligent species.

Once your parrot is comfortable being picked up and held close to the body, it is time to train it to step onto your hand whenever the hand is extended to it.

The parrot is *tamed*.

A couple of footnote observations for the reader. As a general rule, we have found that in order to fully develop this on-off reflex in a parrot, approximately half an hour of repetitious training is the barest minimum needed to achieve the desired results. The object, of course, is to get the bird out of the cage, and that eventually has to be the final test.

Given this on-off training, the reader will be delighted to find that in most cases within forty or so minutes of repetitious trials his pet will be automatically lifting up its foot to meet the extending hand, even if the hand may still be several inches away from it.

A couple of final points to remember. All parrots are either right- or left-footed. The hand should always be presented to the favored side of the bird so that it can more comfortably step up with the appropriate foot. Finally, just as the parrot learns to get on the hand, it simultaneously learns to get off, an important consideration when trying to dislodge a bird which has fallen in love with one's hand.

Chapter 10
Taming Your Medium and Smaller Sized Parrots

TAMING THE MEDIUM SIZED BIRD*

In the previous chapter we loosely defined medium sized parrots as all those birds which approximated the size of an Orange Cheek Amazon, Blue Fronted Amazon, Yellow Head, Red Head, African Grey, and so on. It was also pointed out that the categorization of parrots into large, medium, and small birds was an arbitrary classification designed to assist the first-time bird trainer in taming his parrot in the easiest fashion possible. The master may very well classify his pet as a medium sized bird only to find that it may be difficult to control using the methods outlined in this section. Or, he may find that the bird is small enough to be handled easily by the methods recommended in the later section of this chapter. Whatever the case, if the reclassification of a parrot will simplify taming it, then the master should reclassify it. There will be no loss of effect or success.

To refreshen our reader's recollection, as with the larger parrots, our primary concerns in taming a medium or smaller sized bird can be stated as:

1. To treat the bird with respect and love, always remembering that the creature has suffered nothing but unpleasantness in its relationship with man; to avoid all physical punishments in our

---

*Should the reader have bypassed reading the previous chapter on "Taming Your Larger Parrot," it is highly recommended that it be read before attempting to tame the bird. The total approach, philosophy, and technique are for the most part applicable to medium sized birds and have some bearing on the taming of the smaller sized ones.

This book could never be complete without Ruth and Selsa. While Selsa absolutely loves women, she only tolerates men. Selsa is many things: a little green devil, a rascal, a saucy character and someone who sometimes acts like she is something close to human; but whatever she is at any given moment, she is always Ruth's buddy and companion.

Pedro is a Yellow Crowned Amazon *(Amazona ochrocephala ochrocephala)* owned by Keith Pendell of La Habra, California. Pedro is an absolute darling who will do almost everything expected of him—except be photogenic. Usually he is an affectionate parrot who enjoys humans, but after a long photographic session, Pedro was not his usual affectionate self.

training methodology; to always be aware of the parrot's level of tolerance so that undue stress can be avoided;

2. To tame the bird in a graduated program which will lead it from its state of wildness to a degree of trust and intimacy towards humans; to teach the bird to accept being touched, to being picked up like a kitten with one or both hands around it, to being cuddled and to accept the hand as enough command to get on it when it is offered the bird;

3. To adequately prepare the parrot for its taming sessions by first trimming its wings and talons well in advance of its first taming session; (since the first time trimming and clipping will put the parrot under considerable stress, the master should perform these chores at least a day in advance of the first taming session so that the wild parrot does not go into its first session already unduly pressured).

4. To adequately prepare ourselves by conducting our taming sessions in a room free from distractions; by having a suitable pair of gloves to protect our hands from injury; by having a perch or a facsimile of one for the parrot to stand on.

Because our wild parrot is smaller than most of the species of birds tamed by the previously mentioned method, and since there is less danger of serious lacerations to the hand from most species of medium sized birds, the parrot will be easier to handle and therefore there will be no need for an enclosure. Since all wild parrots will attempt to bite during the initial stages of taming, there will always be the possibility of receiving a painful nip to a finger or hand, an unfortunate but inescapable hazard in the business of taming a wild creature.

Instead of using an enclosure to prevent a difficult-to-handle parrot from escaping and to restrict its movements, our approach with the medium sized bird is to prevent escape and enforce the lesson encounter by physically restraining the parrot by holding it.

After removing the bird from the cage, take it to the training room. It is best to seat oneself in a comfortable chair before beginning the first taming session. Grasp one of the parrot's thighs between the forefinger and thumb in the crook formed between the two fingers. We prefer to hold the parrot in this manner because there is less possibility of injury to the bird's leg during its struggles to free itself. The forefinger and thumb tips, when pressed together, can exert a considerable amount of pressure when holding firm a parrot's lower leg. Should the bird struggle violently, there is always the danger that it may break its leg should the master not release the parrot in time during his zeal to prevent it from escaping. By restraining the bird in this recommended manner, while it is much easier for the bird to escape the hold, there is less possibility of injury.

When seated on the chair it is best to hold the bird as close as possible to the body as permitted under the circumstances.

Obviously, being held fast will not please our terrified bird any more than being restricted by an enclosure pleased his larger cousin. The first few minutes of being held fast will be accompanied by a great deal of violent contortioning, shrieking, growling, and wing flapping. Finding that it cannot escape, the parrot will divert all its attention to the source of its problems and will resort to biting the gloved hand with great vigor. Parrots will sometimes bite with such concentration that it is often quite easy to scratch the parrot's nape and head without the parrot even realizing it. It just continues gnawing no matter what else is happening to it. Should your bird display such concentration on the glove, by all means scratch the head and nape.

Incidentally, the looser fitting the glove, the easier the whole matter of the first one or two sessions will be on the trainer's hand. All the parrot wants to do is free itself, and so anything which appears to be the obstacle preventing freedom will be thoroughly and vigorously gnawed. The parrot is rather indiscriminate in this respect because it does not care what it chews so long as there is something to gnaw at: a finger will do just as well as a piece of leather. A loose fitting glove, however, provides all kinds of chewing material while at the same time preventing the parrot from grabbing onto a sensitive finger.

The chewing behavior is normal. It does not in any way mean that the parrot is some sort of sadist. But should it become lucky enough to find a finger to gnaw on, simply twist the hand towards oneself so that the parrot's head will go downwards. It will usually release the hapless member because the parrot will instinctively attempt to regain its balance. Once repositioned, however, the parrot will again quickly find another part of the glove to chew on.

During this session, begin touching the parrot's back and tail

263

The Yellow Naped Amazon *(Amazona ochrocephala auropalliata)* is a popular pet because of its easy tamability and its predisposition to be a gentle parrot. Indeed, it is a rare Yellow Nape which does not make a good pet. Yellow Napes also rank in the top five best talking parrots.

In 1975 the Geneva Convention recommended that the Vinaceous Amazon *(Amazona vinacea)* be placed on the endangered list, and as such it is not imported into the United States. While the species is reported to enjoy a good temperament and will occasionally breed in captivity, it is doubtful that many bird fanciers will ever have the opportunity to see one.

when it is engrossed in vigorously gnawing at the glove. So long as the parrot is chewing, the back is preferable, but should it object to the back, touch the tail instead. The parrot can rarely twist around far enough to seize a tail toucher.

Parrots constrained and tamed in this manner are always (unfortunately for them) faced with a dilemma. On the one hand, they are prevented from escape by a hand which holds them fast. On the other, something persistently and consistently keeps touching them on the tail and back. Eventually, within a few minutes during its first lesson, it will decide that the hand holding it is the greatest danger. Once it discovers, however, that there is really nothing it can do about being held fast, it will change its priorities again and divert all its concentration to the back toucher.

The parrot will continue changing its priorities as it re-evaluates each new threat. Once the parrot begins perceiving the back and tail touching as an inconvenience at worst, it will again resume the glove gnawing.

That is a good time to begin touching the wings. Of course, the parrot will once more re-evaluate its threat priorities and temporarily postpone the gnawing in order to take a good swipe at the hand. Eventually, as the parrot once more accepts the wing touching for the time being, it will resume its gnawing of the glove, and the trainer can shift the exercise to touching the bird's breast. And so on.

A note of caution. Since the parrot is physically constrained, its violent struggles to free itself will quickly fatigue the bird. Usually, within a matter of a few minutes, the parrot will begin panting heavily. Fatigue and stress should not be confused, however. A reasonable amount of fatigue is a normal reaction to the parrot's struggles. Over-fatigue, however, results in stress. Proper judgment should be exercised so that the parrot is not stressed as a result of overwork. Should the bird continue to *violently* struggle, for example, after ten or so minutes, it is best to conclude the taming session and to return the bird to its cage. Once returned, should the parrot resume its normal activities without much ado, the trainer will have a better idea concerning the parrot's tolerance level of stress. Subsequently, the trainer will be better able to keep future lessons within that tolerance limitation.

As with larger parrots, the lesson as intimated above proceeds in a steady progression of parts of the body touched and eventually accepted by the bird. Tail first, back next, then wings, breast, feet, and head. In this connection, it is usually easy to convince the parrot to accept head scratching and touching because, as noted earlier, the parrot is sometimes so engrossed in gnawing at the glove that it fails to realize that its head is being scratched. Before the bird realizes, it has become conditioned to the head scratching and begins to look forward to more.

Periodically, the trainer should release his hold on the parrot's thigh after the bird begins accepting intimate contact. On the first two or three occasions that the leg is released the parrot will immediately hop to the floor, no doubt overjoyed at having escaped. Should the bird hop down, the trainer should recapture the parrot in as calm and gentle a manner as possible to keep from terrorizing the bird and return it to the former grasp. Should the parrot flee after its release, the trainer should not be dismayed. He will soon find that on one of the occasions of release, the bird will prefer to remain where it is rather than flee.

This is a good time for the trainer to remove the glove from the hand and begin touching the bird. *Moving in as slow and deliberate a manner as possible,* begin the training anew by touching the tail. Once again the bird may show signs of fear towards the *bare hand.* Usually it is quick to learn that an unprotected hand is no greater threat than a gloved one. Actually as the parrot begins accepting the bare hand, correspondingly it develops a fear for the glove. Therefore, few wild birds are handled with bare hands. As a result, most birds soon associate the glove rather than the bare hand with the unpleasantness of being handled. Once the parrot is tamed, the owner will generally find that his parrot, as is the case with many,   becomes terrorized simply by being shown a glove—even from a distance. Some sadistically inclined bird owners find a great deal of amusement in showing a tamed pet a glove in order to elicit the fear reaction, but our position has been that such a practice is unnecessarily cruel.

In beginning the first training sessions by holding the parrot fast instead of placing it in an enclosure, the trainer enjoys certain advantages not found in the other method. Of primary importance is the fact that the bird is held relatively close to the body so that, eventually, it overcomes its claustrophobic reaction to close con-

Once your parrot is accustomed to your touch, frequently scratch its head or neck, caress the bird between its wing and body and gently pat it on the back. Such contacts will help build a strong bond between you and your bird.

Opposite:
When you are training your parrot to walk from hand to hand, your bird might nip you. Parrots often use their beaks as a means to regain their balance, and African Grey Parrots often mouth their owners' hands without meaning any harm.

tact. At the same time the parrot learns there is no danger in being touched, it also becomes accustomed to being near its master.

As with larger parrots, back patting, head and nape scratching, and a forefinger caressing the area between body and wing are immensely enjoyable to the bird. Once the parrot accepts these most intimate of contacts, it is a good practice to use them frequently in strengthening the bond between master and bird. Also, during the frequent rest breaks that should be taken while taming, though still holding it fast (the parrot rarely takes a rest, preferring instead to gnaw at the glove), offer the bird some favorite treat.

Once the parrot accepts the human touch and no longer flees from the hand when released, the bird is taught to walk from hand to hand. This training is a major deviation from the methodology recommended for larger parrots in that instead of teaching the bird to accept being picked up with two hands, the parrot is taught to step from hand to hand.

Because the parrot now accepts being perched on the hand as a matter of course, it is an easy matter to teach it the hand-walking behavior. Our object is to teach the bird to step from one hand onto another in order that it will be much easier to get the parrot to leave its cage or perch on command during the final stages of its training.

Simply push the parrot with the free hand in the area of the breast adjoining the thighs and the bird will step forward in order to keep from losing its balance. Now, with the other free hand, push against the bird. Continue repeating the exercise until the parrot keeps walking from hand to hand as if walking up a ladder.

Should the parrot balk at stepping onto a hand during its first few attempts, or if it hops to the floor, the trainer should not be discouraged. Most medium and small sized birds will start stepping forward in the hand to hand exercise within a few short minutes. Since this is an easy exercise to master and will considerably simplify the final lessons designed to get the bird on the hand on command, we recommend that the trainer perfect this skill in the parrot. This perfection can usually be accomplished within ten minutes or so of steady and constant repetition.

In training the parrot to accept being picked up with two hands (or one hand if the parrot is small enough) and to being cuddled, the procedure outlined in the previous chapter will be the method

Once your bird has learned to accept your hand as a perch, you should begin teaching it to walk from hand to hand.

used for medium sized birds. An enclosure is recommended in order to restrict the bird's movements in the event it should decide that further education is 'for the birds.' As noted in an earlier chapter, small birds tend to be more hyperactive. Some small birds will never permit the kind of intimate contact that comes with being picked up bodily or being cuddled unless, of course, the bird was still a fledgling and hand-raised.

Many larger parrots also refuse this type of intimacy. Should your particular parrot reject all attempts at being picked up with both hands and resent all efforts at being cuddled, then it may be best to forego this aspect of the training. However, it should be stressed that to forego this training should be done only as a last resort. The parrot accepts intimate contact only when it has learned to fully trust man. That trust may come at a later date, perhaps several months after initial training, at which time the trainer may resume this lesson.

Cup both hands gently around the lower portion of the parrot's body, pinning both wings to it. Should the bird become claustrophobic and struggle, immediately release it and repeat the exercise

271

Stepping onto a hand becomes as normal as stepping onto a tree branch in the wilds.

Opposite:
Once your parrot has learned that a hand placed before it is a hand to step on, it will do so.

273

until the bird accepts being enclosed. Once there is acceptance, put a modest upward pressure on the bird's body as if lifting it from the floor but not actually doing so; each time the exercise is repeated the bird should be held a fraction of a second longer before being released. The parrot, regardless of how it may react, will generally not bite if all the previous trainings were adequately completed; namely, if the parrot was tamed by the methods prescribed earlier, it is for all intents and purposes a tamed bird. Therefore, it will not bite out of fear. Should the bird grab onto a finger while it is being encompassed by two hands, all it is trying to do is get enough leverage by which it can free itself.

Eventually, raise the bird an inch or two off of the floor and immediately release it. Repeat the exercise several times, but with each succeeding trial increase the height until finally the bird is being held while you are standing straight. Carry the parrot to another part of the room and release it to the floor.

Carry the bird about the house, each time releasing it after a brief journey from point A to B. With each successive trip, hold the bird ever closer to the body. The final two or three trips can culminate by holding the bird under an arm. It will almost always accept that degree of intimacy by then.

Finally, in teaching the bird to get on and off the hand on command, it is required that there be a continuous repetition of the exercise recommended earlier. Unlike the situation with larger parrots, much of this final battle will already have been won since the bird has already been taught to walk from hand to hand.

Based on our experience, most medium sized parrots can be trained to perform all these functions within two to five hours. Some parrots will take less time than others, and still others will need more time. There is no set rule or pattern applicable to all birds, because the bird's species, its age, the consistency and frequency of training, the disposition of the trainer, and various other variables all influence the rate of learning and taming.

Finally, it should be pointed out, a tamed bird is not a creature which will automatically crave attention, love, and affection. It is not a bird which will suffer unmeasurable agonies just to be with its master. All that the taming procedures have ensured is that the bird will no longer be terrorized by contact with humans and that it will perform various behaviors when they are demanded of it.

A parrot which is loving is a bird which has had a great deal of time devoted to it. It is a creature which is frequently with its master, on his arm or shoulder. It is a creature whose comforts are ensured and who learns to depend on its master.

Succinctly, the intense relationship between bird and man as experienced in the taming session should not end once the parrot is tamed. Otherwise, all that the master will have is a bird which is pretty to look at, which may even be a wonderful mimic, but whose relationship with man will be merely a matter of tolerance.

TAMING THE SMALLER SIZED BIRD

Smaller sized parrots and parrot types are exceedingly simple to tame for a variety of reasons. In the first place, there is no need for gloves, enclosure, or perches. Secondly, because of their size, smaller parrots cannot inflict painful lacerations. Finally, they are so small that they can be easily handled.

In taming smaller sized birds, our objectives remain the same as in training the larger sized ones, but the procedural order of steps involved is somewhat different from that recommended for larger sized parrots. The procedure is different only for convenience reasons. It is as follows:

1. To teach the bird to sit on the finger;
2. To teach the bird to step from one finger to another as in walking up a ladder;
3. To teach the bird to accept being picked up with one hand as in picking up a kitten;
4. To teach the bird to accept being cuddled;
5. To teach the bird to accept the finger enough to get on it whenever required.

The distinct advantage of taming smaller birds is that they are easily managed. While it is true that smaller birds can bite and even draw blood should they seize the right place, the bite is rarely of any consequence. Like bigger birds, small birds are mostly a bag of bluffing feathers which inflict more fear than pain on their masters.

Because smaller parrot type birds are more easily managed and more quickly trained, it is not advisable to attempt to complete the total training in one sitting, although it is possible. As in taming the larger birds, it is strongly recommended that the trainer avoid

275

The African Grey Parrot was first introduced to Europe during the early stages of the Roman Empire. Its talking prowess is as legend today as it was then.

Cockatiels are natives of Australia and have probably become the second most popular pet parrot, following the common budgie. They are friendly creatures which can be extremely loyal to their masters. Sylvester, the author's albino cockatiel, is generally indifferent to most people, but his gray cockatiel, Tweedy Bird, adores men and refuses to even try to tolerate women. Hand her to a woman and she will immediately fly to the nearest man.

using the 'stick method' of finger taming as is often recommended by various manuals outlining parrot taming techniques.

To accept remaining on the hand: Seize the bird with one or both hands, being careful not to injure the wings, and place the bird on the back of one hand. Being frightened, the bird will either attempt to fly away or hop to the floor. Pick the bird up and return it to the hand immediately. After several such adventures, the bird will finally decide that the best course of action is to remain on the hand. If possible, when returning the bird to the hand, encourage the bird to perch on the forefinger.

To step from one finger to another: Once the bird no longer flees the hand, push the free hand's forefinger against the bird's breast where breast and thighs meet. Push hard enough to set the bird off balance. Because the trainee is so small and light, the slightest pressure will upset it and it will step forward in order to regain its balance. Continue repeating this exercise several times. One finger pushes. The bird steps upon it. Now the other free forefinger pushes. Again the bird steps up. The exercise should be repeated in the same pace as suggested by the rhythm of the above instructions while they were being read. The bird will become an expert at this ladder walking within four or five minutes.

Since the smaller bird has no difficulty grasping onto a finger, it will not have to experiment in order to find the right grip for the right place if the forefinger is correctly offered to the bird. As with larger birds, the small fellow may use his beak at first to assist himself in stepping forward to perch on the finger. This is natural and, as the bird acquires confidence, the beak will be infrequently used.

To teach it to accept being picked up with one hand: Because the bird is small, it is easy to accustom the bird to being encompassed by one or both hands. Frankly, even if the bird should never be taught to fully accept this manner of handling, it really doesn't make much difference because all the master has to do is grab the bird with one hand and there is nothing much the little fellow can really do about it when all that is visible of him is a head sticking out of a lightly clenched fist.

278

But for the purpose of developing our bird taming skills, a brief recounting of the method might be helpful. If using one hand, encircle the bird's body with the fingers as if holding the neck of a soft drink bottle; if using both hands, cup the bird in the hands as one would after capturing a butterfly, except that enough space should be left open where the thumbs meet so that the bird can keep his head free. Again, as with the larger birds, the bird's wings should be kept firmly but gently pressed to its body so that should it free a wing it will not struggle to regain a sense of balance.

Of course, the little fellow won't take kindly to this handling and will chirp and squeak a great deal in protest. Unlike larger birds, the small tykes do not sit still when they see a hand reaching down to bodily pick them off the floor. They usually try to scurry away. Fast. But no harm will come to him if the handling is gentle. And so what if he doesn't like it? There is not much he can do about the matter. Most of these tiny fellows eventually come around to where they enjoy such handling, particularly if their head is being scratched at the time.

To teach the bird to accept being cuddled: Once the bird accepts being handled in the manner previously noted, he will accept cuddling. But if he doesn't enjoy being handled that way, make him enjoy it. No reasonable bird can resist having its head scratched. After picking him up with one hand, immediately press him gently to your breast and begin scratching his head and nape. The chirping protests will automatically give way to quiet cheeps of pleasure. Incidently, like bigger birds, the small fellows also enjoy being gently patted on the back as in patting a baby to burp it. While they also enjoy being caressed between wing and body, some judgment is needed here because some of the smaller species can be injured if a large forefinger is inserted between wing and breast. Small fellows are perfectly content if back patting and head scratching are the only caresses they receive. A 'something is better than nothing' philosophy, I suppose.

To accept the finger on command: Finally, all that is required to complete our taming/training is to teach the bird to get on and off the finger whenever the finger is presented to the bird. Since the

This young cockatiel has already become quite used to being handled. Ideally, the taming and training of any bird should begin when the bird is still very young.

The cockatiel invariably proves to be an excellent pet for any household. Because it is a prolific breeder, the cockatiel makes a very fine candidate for anyone wishing to be a hobbyist/breeder.

bird already knows how to step from finger to finger, the training will generally be brief.

Return the bird to the top of its cage and push against the bird as when teaching it to finger walk. Since the bird is so small and so easily managed it has little opportunity to avoid a forefinger which threatens to topple it off of its little wire kingdom. It will very soon learn that the path of least resistance is to step onto the finger. Once it steps onto a finger regularly while sitting on its cage top the exercise should be repeated while the bird is sitting on its perch within the cage. Within minutes, the bird will step off its perch onto a forefinger to be removed from the cage. In removing the little fellow from the cage, be sure to move the hand slow enough at first so that he doesn't bang his head. Most birds have to learn to duck their heads.

In sum, taming a small bird requires very little time or patience. We recommend that on the first lesson the bird be taught to accept the hand, to walk from finger to finger, and to accept being picked up with one or both hands encircling it. The second lesson should quickly recapitulate with a brief practice period what the bird has already learned, and then the bird should be taught to cuddle and to accept a finger on command. Of course, as with the larger birds, the end of the lessons should not be the abrupt end to an intimate relationship between bird and man. The bird will be only as loving as the amount of contact the master is prepared to devote to his pet. While smaller birds rarely display the kinds of overt affection common to larger parrots, they can develop close intimate relationships with their masters if given sufficient opportunity to do so.

Our Half Moon Conure Mo Jo, just as is true of Tweedy Bird, loves to sit on or near this writer's shoulder whenever possible. Open the cage and, lo and behold, they quickly make their way to wherever I may be seated. Perched on my shoulder or on the back of the chesterfield near my head, they are insistent in their demands for attention. And they get it.

Chapter 11
The Mechanics
of Training Animals

All birds have the ability to acquire various tricks and become avid performers if provided the appropriate training. Indeed, parrots, like wild lions, do not even have to be tamed. A wild lion can be trained to perform tricks several times each day before different audiences, but it would never be considered a pet by its trainer because it is a dangerous animal and will always remain so. It simply rejects human companionship. Similarly, while parrots lack the ability to tear off a human's arm or leg, incorrigible parrots can still be taught to become tricksters even though they will never accept the kinds of handling and intimacy which would truly qualify them as pets. As a matter of fact, it would be safe to say that while a wild parrot can be taught to become a skilled performer, it is only the tamed parrot which will usually practice at becoming a "ham" once it has learned various tricks. A good example of a ham would be Fred, the Medium Sulphur Crested Cockatoo trained by Ray Berwick, which regularly appeared on the television program *Baretta*.

There are no dark secrets involved in teaching an animal a trick. The animal learns to master the trick because the trainer employs basic principles as developed by experimental psychology, principles which are used to effectively control the animal's behavior and to elicit from it the kinds of behavior decided upon by the trainer. The creature has no choice in the matter. That is why a wild lion, which might prefer to devour its trainer, leaps through a fiery hoop.

Training an animal or parrot to perform is therefore an entirely mechanical matter, regardless of the creature's success in master-

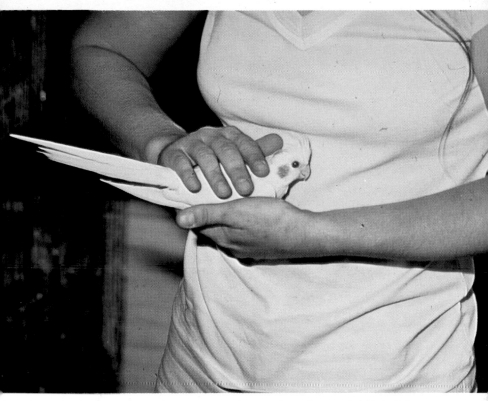

In the long run, no species proves to be as charming and delightful a pet as the cockatiel. While the majority do not talk, they are easy to tame, they take well to people, and they become devoted to their masters. It would be a sorry world for pet owners if there no longer were any cockatiels. As an extra bonus, given their marvelous qualities, they are relatively inexpensive and can be afforded by all.

Opposite:
Even smaller birds like this gray cockatiel will accept confined handling without becoming disturbed. The more time that is spent with the bird after it is tamed, the greater and deeper its trust will be in its master.

ing a particular skill. The trained behavior is mechanical because the animal learns to do it routinely, just as the learning process was a routine matter. For any given situation the animal has at its disposal a variety of different responses which it could make. The trainer's role is to ensure that only certain responses will be performed—those which are essential to the trick—while all others will not occur under that particular situation.

For example, when faced with the flaming hoop, a lion can leap upon its trainer, cower, attempt to flee, growl with terror, bite its tail, jump through the hoop, and so on. The animal can take any of those options when confronted with the flaming hoop, but the trainer's role will be to restrict all possible options to just one: leaping through the hoop. But that task is only part of his role. He must also teach it to jump through the hoop only under certain circumstances, namely when he commands it to. Once the lion has learned *what it is to do* and *under what circumstances,* its behavior has become mechanical for it will no longer be able to exercise any of the options it previously had, such as devouring its trainer when confronted with a fiery hoop.

Most performing animals in zoos and circuses have been taught to perform in the above manner, mechanically. They have not been taught to become pets. That is why, for example, the method of taming recommended in the previous chapter was employed instead of the methods to be discussed in this chapter. By taming the parrot in the manner prescribed earlier, we know that the average bird fancier will be able to develop a relationship with his animal which will not stifle its spontaneity, initiative, and individuality. Its relationship with its master will not be solely a mechanical one, one based on a food reward system.

Before beginning our discussion on the mechanics of teaching a parrot to perform tricks, *it is presupposed that the parrot is already tamed.* A tamed parrot is already manageable and the trainer does not have to worry about handling problems in addition to the problems of teaching a parrot a trick. It is also preferable if the parrot has been taught the meaning of "no," an admonition which is frequently useful in temporarily controlling a parrot's behavior should it interfere with the learning process.

While our primary goal throughout this entire book has been to avoid technical and scientific jargon and explanations, a discussion of some of the principles and processes underlying animal training will be helpful in assisting a trainer in developing a training program for his parrot; it will also be useful in analyzing difficulties which may arise, thereby making it easier to correct them. Some technical terms will be unavoidable, but they will be kept at an absolute minimum and made understandable.

Just as with our wild lion, simple logic tells us that in any given situation there are a number of different ways that a parrot can behave. For example, should we want our parrot to come to us on command and we have decided to use a forefinger held parallel to the perch as its cue (called stimulus, referred to hereafter as S) to come to us, when presenting the finger to the parrot the first time, the bird has a number of alternative choices of behaving (called responses, hereafter referred to as R):

Object: To come forward when presented an S

	Possible R's:
	R1: fly away
	or
	R2: squawk
	or
	R3: stamp foot
	or
S	R4: ignore us
Forefinger parallel to perch =	or
	R5: preen self
	or
	R6: step forward
	etc.

There is only one correct response, of course, and that is to step forward, but *until the bird is taught to recognize the S and to step forward only when the S is presented,* our parrot will continue making inappropriate R's. The process of eliminating these responses is referred to *as conditioning.*

The trick in training the parrot to respond appropriately to the S is to reward it whenever its R approximates what it is supposed to do and to not reward all other R's. In other words, every time

By pushing your parrot in the area of the breast adjoining the thighs, the bird will be "forced" forward in order not to lose its balance.

Opposite:
Now that this Nanday Conure *(Nandayus nenday)* is perched on the hand, it should be trained to walk from hand to hand.

the bird does the right thing, we give it a treat. This process is called *reinforcement.*

If we reward the animal enough times, it will master the trick and our diagram will now look like this:

Object: To come forward when presented an S

$$
\begin{array}{lcr}
\text{S} & & \text{R} \\
\text{(Forefinger parallel} & \text{---- (results in) ----} \blacktriangleright & \text{(stepping forward)} \\
\text{to perch)} & &
\end{array}
$$

R1, R2, R3 etc. are now
excluded from association
with S. They no longer occur.

There is still one more element which needs our consideration before we can begin training our parrot to perform tricks. If we only intend to teach our bird one trick, then there is no need for further consideration of any other variables. But most parrot owners will want to teach their pet a number of different tricks.

The signal which we will use to tell the parrot to do its trick has no reward value in itself. (In our example of teaching the parrot to step forward, it is a forefinger held parallel, but any other S can be used.) Put another way, because we show the parrot a forefinger there is no particular reason why it should do what we want, unless, of course, the parrot is taught that the forefinger represents something special. The situation is identical to the case of a dog which has learned that its food dish represents food; when the dog sees its dish, even when there is no food in it, the dog begins to jump up and down, lick its chops, salivate, and so on. The food dish has come to represent a special significance for the dog. The dog is taught this significance by rewarding it.

Similarly, if we can get our parrot to step forward on the appropriate S, and we reward it every time it does so, the S will come to represent food for the bird. But if we use the forefinger as a sign that food is forthcoming, and use it solely by itself, then any other future tricks that the bird may be required to learn will always have to have the forefinger S presented to the bird in addition to a new signal which will tell the parrot to do its next trick as in hopping onto a stool, for example.

290

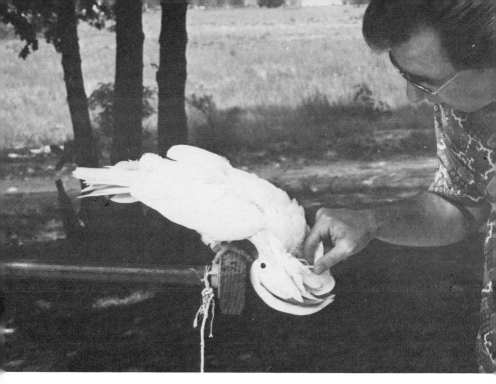

The reward which is used to reinforce a desired behavior is usually a food treat, but the reward could be something else which your parrot enjoys, like having its head or neck scratched.

What is needed, therefore, is a two S system. One S will always tell the parrot, regardless of what trick is being performed, that it is doing the right thing and will immediately be rewarded. The second S will differ from trick to trick, but its primary function will be to tell the parrot what trick is at that time being requested of it.

We, therefore, need to devise a S which can be used with every trick being taught. A sound S is always better than a visual S. (As well, if there are two visual S's, there is always the possibility that the parrot will not see one or both). The sound can be a click sound made with the tongue. It can be a word like "Okay," a word which we prefer. Or it can be another simple word. (The sound should always be simple and uncomplicated.) This sound will become associated with its reward, food.

We also need a new S for each new trick that we wish to teach our parrot. If we will teach it two tricks, we will need two different

Once your pet parrot perches on your hand, it is quite possible that your bird will climb up your arm and onto your shoulder. It is natural for a bird to seek the highest point from which to view its surroundings.

Opposite:
A *tamed* parrot is almost always a trustworthy pet. On countless occasions the introduction of parrots to youngsters has resulted in a love affair between bird and child.

S's. If we teach it five tricks, we will need five new S's (e.g., a fore-finger means step forward; two fingers means hop on the stool; a forefinger held straight upwards means pick up the pencil, and so on). Each S, while also indirectly related to the reward, will become associated with its respective trick.

Hence, when we use the forefinger to tell the bird to step forward, we will also use our common signal "Okay" to tell the bird that it is doing the right thing; when we tell our parrot to hop on the stool when we show it two fingers, we will also say "Okay" immediately after the parrot has attempted the appropriate move; and so on.

In short, then, we will be using two S's with each trick, one S to tell it what to do and the other S to tell the parrot that it is going to get its treat.

Our diagram now, for all practical purposes, will look something like this:

Object: To step forward when presented a S

S1
(finger pointed parallel
  to bird)
    +   (results in)   R
         ————————————————►(stepping forward)
S2 (Okay)

OR

Object: To hop onto a stool.
                 (results in)   R
S1 (two fingers held ——————————► (hopping onto stool)
    parallel to bird)
       +
S2 (Okay)

Now that we have a general understanding of the elements in-volved in training a bird to perform an act, let us briefly review the steps involved in transforming a non-trickster into a performing artist.

For the purposes of illustrating a sample training session, we will train the bird to take *three* steps forward on command when the appropriate S is given the bird. *Only three steps.*

Example 1

Objective: To get the bird to step forward three steps—and *only* three steps—when given the appropriate S.

Stages Involved in training the bird to do this trick:

1. Remove food trays from the bird's cage several hours before the training period is to begin. The parrot must come to the training session hungry—not starved.

2. Choose a room free from distractions.

3. Choose a food for the reward system which the parrot shows a distinct preference for. This food will be used to reinforce its correct R's. The treat must be doled out in small portions.

4. In the beginning, there are basically three ways to get the parrot to make the first correct R:

    a) the bird can be pushed forward one step and then rewarded;

    b) a portion of the favorite food can be placed on the extended parallel forefinger and held a few inches from the bird;

    c) the trainer can just wait until the bird reacts with the correct response.

Alternatives a and b are the best, with b being the preferred method.

5. In using alternative b, the trainer must be careful not to condition the bird so that it will step forward *only* when a kernel of corn is placed on a forefinger. That would blemish the charm of the trick. After the bird has stepped forward two or three times and is successfully rewarded, remove the visible incentive.

6. Each time the bird moves forward, even should it be a quarter

The extremely attractive Golden Conure *(Aratinga guarouba)* is rarely encountered in captivity. A native of eastern Brazil, it is also called either the Yellow Conure or the Queen of Bavaria Conure.

Opposite:
Patagonian Conures make attractive pets. They are rare and not seen often as pets. This fellow, Dominique, loves to ride on the bicycle handles when his mistress does her daily shopping. Dominique was just not interested in being photogenic and quarreled during the entire filming session. He is owned by Laura Gibbons of Balboa, California.

of an inch, *immediately say "Okay"* and *immediately follow that S with its reward.* Through reinforcement, slight moves forward will eventually become a full step.

7. Should the bird step forward when the appropriate S (the forefinger) is *not* shown, *do not reward the parrot.*

8. The parrot will soon learn that by taking one step forward when an S is given there will be an "Okay" (the stimulus tells the bird a reward is coming) which will be immediately followed by a treat.

9. To get the bird to take *two* steps forward, the second stage of the training can *only* begin *after the parrot* has learned to take its first steps in the presentation of the appropriate S.

10. Begin with stage 4b as above. Once the bird steps forward one step, now place its treat on the forefinger holding the hand just a bit from the bird's reach so that it must take a second step in order to receive its reward. Again, the caution in number 5 has to be exercised here.

11. No longer reward the parrot after its first step; *it must be rewarded with an "Okay" and a tidbit only after it has taken a second step or some semblance of a second step.*

12. To teach the parrot to take three steps on command, and only three steps, repeat the procedure as outlined in 9-11.

13. The parrot is never rewarded if it takes four or five steps. It is only rewarded should it take the appropriate number of steps on command S.

Observations

1. The reader will note that the bird learns its trick one stage at a time. Taking three steps, and only three steps, for a bird is a complicated trick. Before it can learn the appropriate trick, it must take first one step upon command, and then take two steps on command, and then it will learn to take the third step on command. When put together and shown a forefinger, the parrot will immediately take three steps forward.

2. It is obvious that the trainer must therefore break each trick into its component parts and treat each successive component separately before the next component can be added to the trick to bring it closer to its successful completion. Learn to think of teaching an

animal tricks as a process in which one building block is placed on another.

3. Once the parrot has learned to successfuly take one step, it is *no longer* rewarded with an "Okay" and a treat *until* it begins taking the second step closer upon presentation of the S. Once the bird has been conditioned to take two steps forward, it is no longer being rewarded until it begins trying its third step.

4. The "Okay" quickly assumes the power of being synonymous with the food reward. In other words, the S "Okay" is associated with food by the parrot like the dog with the empty food dish. The parrot, therefore, responds to it. (Once the appropriate common sound is decided upon, it should never be used with the parrot unless the trainer intends to immediately reward the bird. Otherwise, the power of the S over the bird diminishes.)

5. There will be many trials and errors.

Some Helpful Guidelines

1. S2 (the "Okay") and the reward *must not* be concurrent. First the "Okay" is given, and then the reward *immediately* follows.

2. The "Okay" and the reward must *immediately* follow the attempt by the bird to master its stage (of the trick) or just after its successful completion of it. Long delays equal slow mastery.

3. Any R which resembles the appropriate behavior *must be* rewarded.

4. The animal *must* be hungry.

5. The rewards must be given the parrot in very small portions because the parrot will soon no longer be hungry. A full parrot is generally not interested in becoming an accomplished performer.

6. The reward and the response *must not* compete. That is, the reward comes *only after* the R.

7. By failing to reinforce the behavior, it will become extinct. Simply, the parrot will no longer perform what is expected of it if there is no payoff.

Example 2

Object: To train the parrot to cross the room and give us a kiss.

The Tui Parakeet *(Brotogeris sanctithomae)* is native to Peru and Ecuador. It is only about six inches long, but its green coloring with a patch of yellow and its reddish brown beak make it a lovely small bird.

Opposite:
One of the most colorful of all grass parakeets is the Turquoisine *(Neophema pulchella),* from Australia. It was once feared that this bird had become extinct, but some small, isolated populations were later discovered. Because it breeds well in captivity, it has been saved from extinction.

(The parrot can be taught to either walk or fly over. The training will be almost identical. For the purposes of our example, however, we will train the parrot to walk over.)

Procedure: When presented the appropriate S, the parrot will come across the room when told "Give me a kiss," will step onto an extended arm, the arm will bring the bird to the lips, and the parrot will then give the master a kiss. To accomplish this trick, the following stages of training must be successfully completed.

1. To come forward on presentation of the S (extended parallel forefinger). To give the trick its necessary charm, we will tell the parrot "Give me a kiss" every time we show it the S.

a) Parrot must be trained (as in Example 1 above) to come forward one, two, three, and then many steps. Should the parrot take two steps instead of one, however, it will be rewarded, just as it will be rewarded should it take six steps instead of three. The parrot must be taught to take steps toward us and must not be discouraged from taking many steps because our intent is to get the bird to cross the room.

b) As the bird shows mastery of responding to the appropriate S (and the concurrent "Give me a kiss"), the trainer should move slightly farther from the bird, each time increasing the distance between bird and self, forcing the parrot to cross longer distances in order to be rewarded.

(Caution: Do not overextend the distance between self and bird, for the bird may not be able to discern the appropriate S from the other S's in the room, unless, of course, the parrot becomes also conditioned to the sound of "Give me a kiss.")

c) In successive and gradual steps condition the bird until it can cross several feet of floor when given the appropriate S.

2. To step onto the hand:

a) Hold the arm (showing the S to the bird) parallel to the floor in front of the bird low enough so that the bird can step upward with ease.

b) Hold the other hand (with the reward hidden) slightly above and behind the parallel held arm. (If the parrot is a medium sized bird it would be best to train the bird to step onto the hand and therefore the hand with the reward should

302

be held over its counterpart. Should the parrot be a Macaw sized bird, it would be best for the bird to step onto the forearm and therefore the treat hand should be held accordingly. Whatever it does, however, reward it nevertheless.)

c) The parrot may cross the room but end up standing before the arm. In order to encourage the bird to step onto the hand or arm, the reward can be placed onto the hand so that the bird must step upwards in order to fetch it. As with our earlier caution, this should be done only a very few times until the bird has gotten the idea of what it should do; otherwise the training will go no further than the bird stepping ont the arm and that only if a bit of food is there.

3. To get the bird to give the master a kiss:

a) Once the parrot crosses the room to stand on the arm, and does this regularly without flaw, move the arm *quickly* and *smoothly* to the mouth before saying "Okay" and rewarding the pet.

b) Hold the reward between the lips and allow the parrot to take it. (This requires a bit of smooth operation: while the one arm on which the parrot is being perched is transporting the parrot to the mouth, the lips have no sooner completed saying "Okay" when the other hand places the reward between the lips. The synchronization is not difficult, however.)

(Caution: it is highly recommended that the parrot be tamed for this trick. Otherwise, the trainer may find that his pucker power may not be as good as it once was!)

Some final notes

The last trick is a complicated one, but so are most tricks that are taught various pets. Even the simplest of tricks as conceived by a trainer is a difficult one for a parrot. As much as we may refer to them as being clever and intelligent, most parrots find it difficult and laborious to learn. There have to be many trials and errors, a great deal of patience and time, and a lot of loving and encouragement before a parrot learns to master a given trick. But parrots will learn if the trainer will be patient.

When we see a performing parrot, we marvel at the ease and competence with which the creature performs its skill. We tend

As much as this book is intended for bird fanciers considering a larger bird, it could not be complete without a word or two about the budgerigar *(Melopsittacus undulatus).* While it may be true that a budgie is a budgie, the budgie is by far the most popular of parrots and parrot-types. This little fellow, owned by Norma Robinson, was totally wild five minutes before the filming session. After the author had asked Norma to pose for the picture, she received a bite on her cuticle when she tried to remove her budgie from his cage. "Must I smile with this thing?" she asked as she tried to restrain it so that its wings could be clipped. Five minutes later Mr. Budgie was perfectly content to sit on her finger. No wonder these birds are popular.

The budgie has adapted well to captive breeding. Indeed, because of the many mutations in its pattern and colors, breeders have capitalized on this natural diversity to breed a variety of colorful strains, all to the delight of budgie fanciers.

Remember that the food treat should be placed between your lips as soon as you finish saying "Okay."

to forget the effort that went into the parrot. The amount of effort required to produce a performer, however, can be reduced if the trainer uses the 'building block approach' to the problem to be learned. By analyzing the overall trick to determine the component parts, a great deal of frustration can be avoided by both bird and man. Should the training bog down at some point, then it is time for the trainer to re-examine his training program. Almost always the problem results from a situation in which there may be three or four individual skills to be mastered separately as in the building block approach, but in failing to completely dissect the trick into its component parts, the trainer is expecting the parrot to master those three or four skills simultaneously. Such a situation may be just too difficult for a parrot to handle.

In the following chapter are a number of tricks which can be taught to both large and small parrots and parrot types. Some tricks may be more appropriate for the larger birds and some for the smaller ones. The tricks are only a few examples of what can be done with parrots. The kinds of things which can be taught a pet parrot are limited only by the size and intelligence of the bird and by the reasonable expectations of the master. All that is needed is a bit of imagination.

Good luck, wild lion tamer!

The driving of the truck by this Green Winged Macaw is a complicated trick which requires many hours of conditioning. Pet fanciers wishing to train their birds to perform such stunts should begin by first teaching their pets far simpler tasks. Once the parrot *learns* to *learn*, then more complex tasks can be taught to the bird with less effort.

Opposite:

Even though Gypsy is fifty or so years old, she has proved to be a highly intelligent Scarlet Macaw. Like all other Scarlets, she is capable of learning late in life. Gypsy learned to skate when she was in her forties, and today she is a regular performer at Lion Country Safari in Laguna Hills, California. Gypsy is owned by Bob Branch of Garden Grove, California.

Chapter 12
Teaching Your
Parrot to do Tricks

As much as we love our pets and we like to think of them in human terms by describing them as intelligent or smart, we soon find that when we begin training them they do not always learn as quickly as we somehow imagined they would. Teaching the parrot a trick proves to be a painstaking and laborious process involving many trials and errors.

But if we are patient, our parrot will indeed learn to perform his tricks. The first one will always be the hardest, but each succeeding trick will be just a bit easier for the bird to master. While the trick itself is something that both the parrot and his trainer can be proud of once it is mastered, there is always that good feeling which comes from working with the pet and strengthening the bonds which were already developed during its taming period.

All the love and the patience in the world will be of little use, however, if the trainer does not adequately prepare himself by doing his homework before working with his pet: each of the component parts of the trick must be identified and the means of teaching the parrot each component part must be decided upon. With simple tricks, there will not be many decisions to make and the parrot will soon learn what it is supposed to learn. With the more complex tricks, more time will be needed but if the various components are properly identified, there will always be a feeling of accomplishment at the end of a lesson as the parrot masters another part or two of the trick.

Finally, once again, it is always best that the parrot already be tamed beforehand. A tamed bird is easier to handle and, already having developed a working relationship with its master, it will work hard to please him. Of special importance, moreover, is the fact that if our parrot is already tamed, the problem of stress need not be worried about so long as we keep the training sessions within reasonable limits and not over-fatigue the bird. The last important point to remember is to be sure that the parrot is hungry when it begins the lesson. We love our pets and it is always difficult to take away our pet's food dish when we know that it will soon be looking for something to eat. No one likes to keep his pet hungry, but hungry it must be if it is to learn a trick.

The various tricks in the following section of this chapter are only a few skills that a trainer may wish to teach his parrot. They are by no means the only tricks that can be taught a bird, and their inclusion in this book does not in any way mean that they are the best tricks. But they are tricks which are relatively uncomplicated and which have proven themselves easy for both master and pet. As the reader develops his skills in conditioning parrots to perform, he can use his imagination to devise other tricks.

THE SMART ALECK BIRD

Object: To teach the parrot to answer a question with either a "Yes"or "No."

(This trick can always be used for comedy results with good effect because strange questions can be given the bird and incongruous answers received in return. In a room full of little girls, for example, the parrot's "Yes" answer to "Do little girls eat snails?" will be sure to elicit giggles and laughter.)

Procedure: When given the appropriate S, the parrot will shake its head for a "No" answer, and if given another S, the bird will nod its head for a "Yes" reply. The question itself is irrelevant for it is used only for effect. The parrot learns to respond to the hand signal and not to the question.

The trick is actually two tricks and not one.

The "No" Response

1. Put the parrot on a standing perch.
2. To get the parrot to shake its head for a "No" answer, put a

This photograph clearly shows how strong a macaw's beak is and how the macaw, as with other parrots, uses its beak almost like a third foot.

Blue and Gold Macaws are one of the most popular and intelligent macaws, rivaling only the Scarlet in price and availability. This fellow, called Easy, is a regular performer at Lion Country Safari in Laguna Hills, California. He plays dead, says his prayers, high jumps and is capable of riding a bicycle. Easy is owned by Bob Branch.

small piece of tape approximately one-half-inch-square at the back of the parrot's head. The parrot will attempt to get rid of the tape by shaking its head. (Should the parrot keep turning its head, making it difficult to put the tape in place, divert its attention with a treat held in the other hand.)

3. As soon as the parrot shakes its head "Okay" reward it.

4. Immediately remove tape. (Otherwise the parrot, upon consuming its treat, may get involved in a life and death struggle to remove the tape, thereby interfering with the lesson).

5. Replace the tape and repeat as before; the parrot will soon begin looking forward to its treat.

6. Introduce the appropriate hand signal. Reward the parrot only when it shakes its head when the signal is present.

7. As the parrot begins responding to the hand signal, try the signal without the use of the tape. Reward only head shaking behavior when the tape is absent. Should the parrot balk and not shake its head after a few attempts, return to step six before trying again.

8. Once the bird begins shaking the head appropriately to the hand signal, accustom the bird to the sound of a question being asked concurrent to the presentation of the signal. Keep the sound of the voice low keyed and vary the questions so that the bird will become accustomed to the inflection at the end of the sentence and not to a specific question.

The "Yes" Response

1. Place the parrot on a perch.

2. Put a piece of the bird's treat on the hand which will be showing the bird the appropriate signal (e.g. a closed fist with a kernel of corn on the back of the fist).

3. Hold the hand several inches from the bird's beak. The hand should be presented to the bird at approximately the perch's height. If the reward is held close enough to the parrot, he will reach downwards and try to get the treat.

4. Immediately "Okay" the bird and reward it.

314

5. Continue repeating until the parrot begins to show signs that it is beginning to understand what it is supposed to do. Once it does, no longer show the bird the treat that is in store for it (otherwise the parrot will become conditioned to nodding only when its treat is placed on the hand held in front of it).

6. Begin introducing different questions each time the signal is given the bird.

Having learned this aspect of the trick, the trainer should now be able to ask the parrot any question and obtain the appropriate response. (An interesting aspect of the charm of this trick is that the parrot will not respond to anyone else's question, unless of course, the other person learns what signal to give the bird).

POTTY TRAINING

While this is not a trick in the real sense of the word and, to confess, this writer has yet to set out and teach a parrot to be potty trained, we have decided to include it in this section nevertheless.

Friends of the author, Helen and Dave Schuelke of Westminister, California, have a White Cockatoo, often called the Umbrella Cockatoo, named Babe who is completely toilet trained. Should the bird be out of its cage and on the carpet, for example, it will return to its cage area and pace back and forth until it is picked up and returned to its perch. Only then will it go about its toilet business. As explained to this writer, their procedure was as follows:

1. It is essential that the parrot know the meaning of "No" and that it responds to the admonition.

2. When it has been observed that the parrot has defecated, remove the parrot from the cage twenty or so minutes later. If possible, hold the bird perched on the arm until it is prepared to defecate again. If the parrot finds it difficult to sit still until its next bowel movement, amuse the bird by caressing it or using whatever means possible to keep the parrot close at hand. The parrot and trainer should be situated near the cage.

Parrots defecate frequently, particularly younger birds, and so in most cases the trainer will not have to wait too long before

Trained parrots are always a source of enjoyment and wonder, particularly for children. More often than not, the birds themselves seem to enjoy performing their stunts.

Here a macaw proves just how intelligent a macaw can be. Not only must he pick up an object and put it down some place else, but he must also match each object with a hole of a particular shape.

Some bird trainers do their trick training outdoors, but this is not always a safe thing to do. It requires a very tame bird, and the bird's wing(s) must be clipped. Care must also be taken that nothing (for example, stray animals) can harm your parrot.

Nature calls again. (It is easy to tell when a parrot is going to defecate because the bird will make a squatting motion and lift up its tail.)

3. As soon as it appears the parrot is going to defecate, *loudly* and *immediately* say "No," push down on the tail, and *immediately* return the parrot to its cage. (It is important that the tail be pushed down because by lifting the tail upwards, the muscles in the vent area are relaxed enough for Nature to do her work. Keeping the tail down therefore makes it difficult for the bird to eliminate.)

4. Since the bird must defecate, it will do so as soon as the pressure is released off its tail once it has been returned to its cage. Okay it and give it a treat.

5. Repeat this procedure until the parrot learns to defecate in its cage. It may be necessary to work with the bird for several days, two or three hours a day, before it learns the trick.

While it should be remembered that the object is not to teach the parrot to defecate on command, the parrot can be taught to do so, as Babe so clearly demonstrates. The object is to teach the parrot that the couch, shoulder, or floor is not an appropriate place to leave dirt.

318

THE ACROBAT

We first heard of this trick while reading the Bates and Busenbark book, *Parrots and Related Birds*. The authors mentioned hearing of a parrot which enjoyed being swung around the head on a rope. We first tried this stunt with Selsa and found that she not only learned to perform it within a few minutes, but that she also seemed to enjoy it. We have since then taught a number of parrots this trick with equal results.

Object: To teach the parrot to hold onto a rope while being swung around the head. (There is no need to develop a hand signal for this trick. The rope will adequately serve as the parrot's cue to perform.)

Procedure:

1. A piece of rope approximately half an inch in diameter and five to six feet long is required. The rope must be coarse and thick enough so that the parrot can hold onto it easily without slipping or losing its hold when subjected to centrifugal forces. (Just in case, it is always a good idea to tie a simple knot at the end of the rope where the parrot will be holding on.)

2. The parrot must be taught to grab hold of his end of the rope. Offer the parrot the knotted end of the rope. As soon as the parrot takes the rope in its beak or foot, Okay and reward it. The parrot will soon learn that the rope is synonymous with a treat whenever he takes hold of it.

3. The parrot must be taught to hold onto the rope while it is being swung.

   a) With the parrot holding to the knotted end, lift the bird a few inches off the floor and gently swing it back and forth. Parrots are accustomed to this kind of acrobatics while in the wild, and so this part of their training will be familiar to them.

   b) Slowly turn around in circles so that the parrot is also going around in circles a few inches off the floor. The circles should be fast enough so that enough centrifugal force is exerted to swing the bird a few inches off the floor, but not too fast in the beginning because the parrot may become frightened and lose its hold on the rope. (By doing these first

319

Babe is an Umbrella Cockatoo *(Cacatua alba)* owned by Dave Schelke of Garden Grove, California. (It was Dave who shared with the author the method for potty training a bird.) Prior to the filming, Dave told Babe to "Go potty. Go potty"—which the bird promptly did. Babe also gives kisses and will snuggle his head against Dave's chest when told to "Give me love." Babe, like most other tamed parrots, hates gloves. In order to get a picture of Babe with his crest up, he had to be distressed by being shown a glove. It worked.

320

few practices just a few inches off the floor, there is less possibility of injury should the bird let go of the rope.)

c) This following stage of training should be done outdoors because there will be considerable centrifugal force exerted on the bird and until the parrot learns to hold onto the rope securely, there is always a danger of the bird losing its hold and crashing into a wall should the training be done in the home.

Gradually begin increasing the distance between the ground and the parrot until the bird is being swung around the head at head level and in a five- or six-foot diameter circle. There is no need to turn one's body; the rope can be easily swung around the head. The proper speed should be just enough to maintain the bird at the same altitude with each swing.

Once the trick is over and the rope is at rest, the parrot generally needs a few seconds to recover from being dizzy. We hold the parrot on his end of the rope a few inches off the floor and once it has recovered its sense of balance, we encourage the bird to climb up the rope to our hand. The parrot will usually climb up the rope by itself, but we train them to climb up with a snap of the fingers and a reward. Once perched on the hand, we finish off the performance with a kiss.

The trick is especially charming if the parrot has been conditioned enough so that it will immediately come to its master whenever the master is holding onto the rope. The appeal, of course, is that the bird wants to perform.

HOWDY PARTNER

Object: To teach the parrot to shake hands.

Procedure: Since all parrots show a predisposition to be either right-or left-footed, it is best to teach the parrot to shake hands with the foot which it is most accustomed to using. (This can be easily ascertained by observing what foot the bird uses in feeding or when first stepping onto a perch.)

1. Put the parrot on a perch.

2. The parrot must be taught to lift one foot off the perch and to move it up and down as in a waving motion.

a) A good signal to use is a forefinger pointed at the parrot. Since the parrot must grab something if it is to shake hands, the forefinger can be used for the shaking hands routine, as the appropriate signal and as a means of teaching the parrot what to do.

b) Hold a forefinger pointed diagonally toward the parrot just out of its reach. (It is best that the bird already be trained to step onto a hand on command so that the reflex is automatic. If so, less time will be needed for the parrot to master this trick.)

c) When the parrot reaches for the finger as to step on it, slowly move the finger upwards. As soon as the parrot's foot follows, Okay and reward it. (It is important that the movement be slow enough; otherwise the parrot's foot may not follow a fast moving finger. It is also important to keep the parrot from touching the hand.)

d) Continue rewarding the parrot every time its foot follows the finger when the finger is presented to the bird. As the bird becomes accomplished at this, move the hand up and down two or three times before rewarding the bird.

e) Increase the number of upward and downward foot movements to five or six, which will make the handshake more realistic. While the parrot's foot may instinctively follow the finger two or three times, it may not follow more than that. It may be necessary to add one movement at a time to the parrot's pumping action until the bird has the required number conditioned into its repertoire.

f) Gradually increase the tempo of the up and down movement so that it more closely approximates the pumping action speed of a handshake.

Once the parrot automatically shakes its foot up and down on presentation of the cue, it must be taught to hold the finger while at the same time pumping it up and down;

a) When the parrot reaches outwards on presentation of the finger, and *before* it begins to pump its foot, put the finger in the bird's foot.

b) The sensation of the finger in the foot may temporarily disorient the parrot so that it may not pump its foot as expected. If so, move the foot up and down the required number of pumps and (⟶ ard the parrot. The bird will soon get the connec ⟶ t does, allow the parrot to do the pumping.

c) All handshakes must eve ⟶ d and the hands must eventually be released. After his ⟶ ke pump, the parrot may continue to hold the finger. ⟶ ithhold the reward until the parrot lets go. The bird c ⟶ ncouraged to let go immediately after the handshake by ⟶ ng it the treat held just below it. If the parrot has to re ⟶ n to get its treat, it will need both feet on the perch ⟶ n lets go of the finger to get its reward. Okay and re ⟶ t.

d) Of course, the charm of the t ⟶ to say "Shake hands" when presenting the parrot w ⟶ cue. The bird will shake another person's finger so lo ⟶ he bird sees the appropriate cue from the trainer. All th ⟶ er has to say is "Shake hands with Mary" and so long a ⟶ gives the parrot a forefinger, the parrot will pump it

DEAD BIRD

Object: To hold the bird in the hand whil ⟶ lying on its back. *Procedure:* It is important that the bird be t ⟶ and that it will accept handling. Unless the bird has learned ⟶ ist its master, the Dead Bird trick will be difficult to teach a ⟶ ot.

1. Teach the bird to accept having its back ⟶ hed and the hand encompassing it from the back. (Should the ⟶ ot already accept this degree of intimacy as a result of its tam ⟶ move on to stage two.)

a) Perch the parrot on one hand;

b) To get the parrot to accept having th ⟶ nd with palm down touching its back, briefly touch the b ⟶ nd then Okay and reward it.

c) As the parrot accepts being touched, ir ⟶ se the length of time that the palm rests on the back befc ⟶ ewarding the parrot.

d) Encompass the bird's body with the ⟶ d. (A second person will be needed to reward the bird bec ⟶ e both hands will now be occupied.) Continue reinforcing ⟶ bird's acceptance of the encompassed hand.

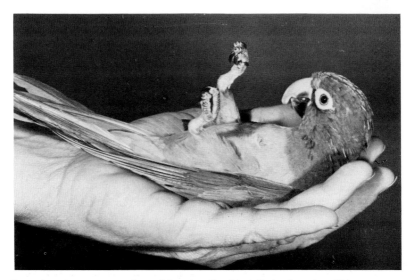

Despite the unnatural position for the bird, "playing dead" is an easy trick for most parrots to learn.

e) Increase the period of time that the parrot will accept being encompassed to several seconds. The parrot should allow the hand to hold it across the back without moving.

2. The parrot must be conditioned to lie still on its back while being held in the palm of one hand.

a) With the bird perched on one hand, place the other hand around the parrot's back and tilt the bird slightly backwards. The tilting may alarm the bird due to its loss of equilibrium, so do not tilt the parrot too far backward at first. Since both hands are occupied, have the helper reward the parrot. The trainer should say Okay, however.

b) Continue tilting the parrot backward in increasing increments, being sure to Okay and reward the parrot during each tilt.

c) This exercise should continue until the parrot will accept being tilted and lying flat on its back in the palm of the hand.

d) Once the parrot accepts lying on its back, increase its tolerance for this unnatural position by delaying the time between the second the bird is finally prone and the time it is

324

Okayed and rewarded. Do not expect too much too fast at this stage of the bird's training because the position is totally unnatural for the bird.

While it is conceivable that a parrot could be taught to remain on its back for several minutes, there is really no need for that. A parrot which is 'dead' for ten or so seconds is a well-trained parrot.

3. The parrot must be taught to release its hold on the hand.

a) Once the parrot lies on its back without problems, have the helper gently pry one foot free from the hand. Okay and reward. After several such pryings, the parrot will soon learn that it will not receive its reward until that foot is free.

b) Repeat the same procedure with the second foot.

c) The parrot will soon learn to lie on its back and, on doing so, immediately release its grasp of the hand. (Some trainers push the bird's two feet together so that they will grasp each other, thereby satisfying the parrot's reflexive need to grasp onto something, but such a bird doesn't look quite as dead as a parrot with both feet upward.)

4. The parrot must be taught to let its head hang while it is prone on its back when given the command 'play dead.'

a) A good cue is the phrase 'play dead.'

b) When the bird is on its back, have the helper push the bird's head slightly downward after giving the command 'play dead.' As soon as the head is pushed downwards, Okay and reward.

c) In increasing increments, continue pushing the head further backward until it will hang there upon command.

DINNER'S READY

Object: To train the bird to come to its master at the sound of a bell.

Procedure: Whenever the bell is sounded, the parrot will either fly across the room (if unclipped) or walk across the room to a food dish. The trick has special appeal if the trainer says "Come and get your dinner" before ringing the bell.

1. The parrot must be taught to cross the room upon presentation of the appropriate cue. In this case, it will be a bell. See Example 1 in the previous chapter for the exact procedure. There are some slight differences, however:

   i) a bell is substituted for a hand signal (ring the bell only once instead of a number of times, keeping the cue as simple as possible);

   ii) as part of its training, the parrot must stand before a food dish before it receives its Okay and reward. There is no problem here, for as the bird learns to come across increasing distances and the food dish will always be just in front of the trainer, the parrot will soon associate the food dish and its position relative to it as part of the appropriate behavior for a reward;

   iii) do not put the reward in the food dish;

   iv) plan your strategy so that the training will involve crossing the room to a particular place where the food dish will always be found should the bell be rung.

2. Once the parrot crosses the room upon hearing the bell, it must stand before the food dish until it is rewarded. However, the object is for the parrot to cross the room, *wait patiently by the tray for some food,* and then eat it when the food is dropped into the tray.

If the bird is reinforced by putting food in its tray each time it learns to cross greater distances to the tray at the sound of the bell, but the food is placed in the tray before the parrot gets there, it will immediately put its head into the tray. Much of the charm will have therefore been lost. The solution is to wait two or three seconds before putting the treat in the dish. A note of caution, however. If the delay between the behavior and the reward is too great, the behavior will become extinct.

With this kind of trick, quaint routines can be developed as in the following example.

"Dinner is ready. Come and get it."

The bell is rung.

The parrot crosses the room to stand before the dish.

The parrot, if already taught how to nod "Yes," can now be asked "Do you want some dinner?"

The parrot nods.

The food is placed in the dish.

326

Chapter 13
Teaching a Parrot to Talk

The one distinctive quality about parrots which distinguishes them from all other household pets is the uncanny ability of some parrots to imitate human sounds. While various animal species can be taught a variety of tricks—some of them often complex and seemingly beyond the physical and mental ability of the animal—it is only the parrots and parrot types which can be taught to talk and sing in addition to performing tricks.

Yet while talking ability is a common denominator to most species within the family of parrots, not all parrots and parrot type species talk, and some species rarely if ever produce individuals capable of imitating human sounds. Some species, on the other hand, are internationally recognized as talkers and are therefore highly prized for this ability. African Grey Parrots, Mexican Double Yellow Heads, and Yellow Naped Amazons are among the three best candidates if a talking bird is desired.

Some aviculturists argue that only the African Grey and Mexican Double Yellow Head can be classified as good talkers. There is considerable evidence, however, to dispute this claim. Another major controversy, of course, centers around which species is the best talker. Preferring to remain outside this emotional and polemical exercise, suffice it to say that each species has its advantages and disadvantages. African Greys are more sedate birds and, unlike Amazons in general, they don't go on periodic shrieking rampages. Unfortunately, however, they are generally not very affectionate or personable. Yellow Heads, on the other hand, can be exceptionally personable and affectionate, but they do tend to insist on having one or two healthy shrieking sessions per day. The ideal Yellow Head is a parrot which is an excellent talker and a personable bird, but many Yellow Heads lack one or the other of these two desired qualities. Yellow Napes are pleasant birds but tend to lack the colorful personality and behavior of Yellow Heads and the air of wisdom that Greys seem to have about them. In short, there is no ideal bird.

While almost all parrots and parrot types are natural imitators of some sounds common to their environment, the degree to which they will successfully imitate various sounds is dependent on a wide range of factors. The age of the bird is one critical variable. Most parrots with talking ability can learn to talk up to about their fifth year of life. Birds older than that are difficult to train if they have not already learned some words. Some parrots, surprisingly, may never utter a word for three or four years and then suddenly, to everyone's astonishment, begin uttering words and phrases.

The best candidates for talking are obviously young birds, preferably chicks without their full complement of feathers. Young parrots are more flexible, more apt to associate themselves with their masters, and less inclined to assert their independence. But even so, just because a parrot is extremely young is no guarantee that it will talk, even should it belong to a species recognized as talkers. And conversely, there are innumerable accounts of various parrots considered poor candidates for talking which have astounded their masters with extensive vocabularies even though there was no concerted effort taken to teach them to talk.

While the age of the bird as well as its species is a critical variable in talkability, the character and disposition of the parrot are just as important. There are individual differences between one bird and another within a given species which account for one parrot talking and the other not, all other factors being equal. The younger the bird, however, the less opportunity there is for the bird to develop personality characteristics which inhibit learning processes.

Some people seem to believe that parrots learn to talk as naturally as they learn to fly. While there are some exceptional individuals which learn to talk with little or no coaching, the great majority of all talking parrots acquired their skills because of a persistent teacher. A parrot imitates a sound because that particular

Young parrots would be ideal 'voice students,' but not all parrots have the same potential for talking. These young cockatiels might learn to mimic some human sounds, but they probably would never learn to mimic words to the extent that an African Grey parrot can.

sound was repeated time after time. Before a parrot will imitate a sound the teacher must expend great effort, time, and patience in training the bird to talk. Until the bird finally learns the word, there is nothing but disappointment. Quite often a master repeats a word fifteen or twenty times in a row—which after the fifth time seems like the fifteenth million time—and tires of the monotony, boredom, and disappointment. After a week or so of such sporadic and ineffectual training, the master finally concludes that the parrot will never talk and hence forgoes any further training. Experience suggests that the trainer's impatience is often the deciding factor whether a bird capable of talking eventually learns to speak.

Sometimes, after a parrot begins to learn to talk and masters several expressions, it is no longer given any further lessons.

Many species and individual birds have the ability to master far more than the few words they have acquired but their full potential is never realized because the training has ceased.

The conditions under which a parrot is expected to learn his lessons also determine the final results. In order for a parrot to learn a word, the repeated sound must somehow penetrate the creature's consciousness. If there are twenty children running about the house screaming in their play, if the television is blaring, if the vacuum cleaner is humming, no one sound from that hodgepodge makes itself impressionable on the parrot.

A parrot learns best when it enjoys a good working relationship with its master. A parrot which finds pleasure with its master and which prefers to be in its master's company is a bird whose attention can easily be captured.

Finally, not all parrots learn at the same pace. Some parrots may learn their first word after only a short period of repetition, while others may learn that same first word only after several weeks or even months of constant repetition. But once the word has been learned, regardless of how long it has taken the bird, the master can rest assured that *the parrot has the ability* and that all that is now required is persistence and patience. One of the biggest hurdles has been conquered. With each succeeding word mastered it becomes increasingly easier for the parrot to master the next word.

Just as there are a wide range of variables determining whether a parrot will talk or not and determining the range and extensiveness of the vocabulary, there are distinctive differences in the quality of the imitation of the mimicked word. As observed earlier, the smaller the bird the squeakier the voice and the less accurate is the imitation of the actual sound.

While not necessarily always true, our experience has shown that when a parrot known for its talking capabilities has a genuinely warm relationship with its master to the extent that it enjoys its relationship with its master and is a willing student for taming and training, it also generally tends to be a good candidate for talking. Parrots which are friendly and amenable are parrots which have learned to be attentive—otherwise they never would have been tamed. As a matter of fact, a bird which readily responds to taming and training is a bird which reflects a specific

330

unique quality about its personality. Yet not all friendly birds learn to talk and, indeed, some ornery and mean parrots sometimes learn to talk well.

Parrots show a remarkable propensity for developing a preference for one sex or another and for one person or another, sometimes even to the exclusion of all others. Selsa shows a preference for females, for example. While Ruth can do virtually whatever she wishes with that parrot, no matter how obnoxious that treatment could be, the parrot will accept it without biting. Not that we are harsh with our birds; we have only tested her tolerance levels to men and women.

Men, however, are barely tolerated, although she will permit this writer to engage in modest degrees of intimacy with her. Selsa, simply speaking, accepts all women and barely tolerates men.

On the other hand, Tweedy Bird, our gray Cockatiel, shows a marked preference for men. Sylvester, her cage mate, makes no distinctions whatever based on sex. Sylvester, however, is somewhat of an exception because most birds do show a preference eventually.

It has been suggested that parrots generally prefer women to men. The rationale is that parrots like women because women have softer voices, are gentler with birds, and are the ones who daily feed and care for the bird. There might be merit in this argument if it weren't for the fact that some men have extremely harsh voices and manners and never feed their birds, but they are preferred by their pet parrot often to the total exclusion of their spouses.

This author has no suitable answer which might explain this problem. All that he can suggest is that if one's favorite parrot takes a special liking to one's spouse, the best thing to do is swallow one's injured pride and learn to live with it.

Most certainly a talking bird is a joy and an endless source of amusement, entertainment, and pride for its masters. While disappointment is understandable should one's parrot never perform according to the real and imagined reputation we impose on the creature, if the bird is a friendly, warm being then credit should be given where credit is due. A talking parrot which has little or no tolerance for man is a creature locked in a cage mimicking this or that. In the beginning, the mimicry is a source of amusement, but

Macaws are one of the few parrots which can be taught to perform tricks *and* be taught to talk.

332

the bird always remains outside of the family circle. It remains locked in its cage, like prized china in a cabinet, something to look at but something which eventually loses its appeal because no one can touch, admire, or fondle it.

A friendly parrot, however, is always an interacting individual whose everyday activities change as the parrot gets involved with one mischief after another. It is a creature which can be fondled, which is warm to the touch, which responds in a multitude of ways to its master.

But should a parrot be a vital and friendly creature and one which also talks, so much the better.

There is no mystery involved in teaching a parrot to talk. A sound is presented repetitiously to the bird over a period of time until the parrot begins attempting to imitate that sound. Parrots will often imitate certain words at the total exclusion of any other words presented for learning. Sometimes a parrot will imitate a word or phrase once or twice and never repeat it again. It is difficult to understand why one sound may be preferred to another, but all other factors being equal, perhaps it is because certain sounds, words or phrases are either too unappealing or too complex for a particular bird.

While it could be argued that there are similarities between teaching a parrot to talk and teaching it various tricks, there are significant differences between the two in the amount of effort expended and the observable results. Most tricks taught to parrots are, relatively speaking, simple, requiring no more than a few hours at most. For example, most Amazons can be taught to hand walk within a few minutes, and most Amazons can be taught to shake hands in two or three hours. After a few minutes, the trainer can observe progress in his student's mastery of the skill being tried.

When taming a parrot or teaching it to perform a trick, the trainer works as hard as the pupil. With each succeeding attempt the parrot makes to master a task, it improves its performance and the results are observable.

When training a parrot to talk, however, the master's patience and persistence are essential to the learning process because there are fewer indications that the parrot is attempting to mimic the sound, and a much longer time is required before results can be observed. Also, when using live voice training methods, a great deal of concerted effort is required. Moreover, while most parrots and parrot types can be taught at least the simplest of tricks, the majority of parrots will never learn to mimic even the smallest of words. In other terms, the trainer may expend a great deal of effort, patience, and persistence without any results or with a minimum of results.

The reader might conclude that additional perseverance and effort will result in fruition. He might conclude that a word should be repeated every few seconds throughout the bird's waking hours. Such constant and incessant repetition, unfortunately, becomes nothing more than just another fixture in the parrot's environment. A parrot responds to a word because the bird is attentive to the sound. A sound which is constant generally fails to command the parrot's attention.

METHODS OF TRAINING

There are two basic approaches which can be taken to teach a parrot to talk. One method is to purchase a recording which has been especially prepared for teaching parrots and is played on a record or cassette player. The second method is for the trainer to constantly repeat the particular word to the parrot until the bird begins imitating the live voice. These are the only two methods. There are no more. There are some people who believe there is a third method: they believe that by splitting the parrot's tongue the bird will immediately begin imitating human sounds. Parrots talk because of the peculiarities of their voice boxes and not because they manipulate their tongues as do humans. Not only is the splitting of a parrot's tongue unnecessary and likely to lead to consequences detrimental to its health, but tongue splitting is unnecessarily cruel and barbaric.

There are a variety of commercial records available in pet shops which are inexpensive and which can be used to teach the parrot to talk. These records can simplify teaching because no further effort is really required except that of purchasing and playing them until results are realized.

There are, however, various drawbacks to them which in this writer's opinion make them less than desirable. In the first place the records always have several words and expressions imprinted on each side, the number ranging from seven or eight to as many as twenty different words. Regardless of the order in which they are presented, the records are never totally satisfactory because no one word is repeated any significant number of times in the course of each daily lesson. This is especially important when the parrot has yet to learn his first word.

Furthermore, commercial records present words and phrases in varying degrees of difficulty. While one side of the record may begin with a word as simple as "Hi," it may end that side's lesson with an expression as complex as "This Polly hates crackers." Before the parrot has even begun mastering the "Hi" it is already confronted with a more difficult learning problem.

There are other deficiencies in using commercial records. They encourage the trainer to rely on the record to produce results. In doing so, the master becomes removed from the learning process and is less likely to intervene in assisting the parrot to learn at a pace which is best for it.

Of special concern is the fact that commercial records are produced by entrepreneurs who have decided for themselves *which* words and phrases would be best for parrots to learn. They are prepared with the intention of appealing to the buyer's ear more than to the problems related with teaching a parrot to talk. In that way they are like fishing lures in a tackle store: they capture a lot of fishermen, but they rarely catch fish.

While a parrot owner can very well interject new material extraneous to that presented by the record and teach the parrot some one expression which is unique, the parrot will have acquired various expressions which are common to all other parrots. It may be cute for a parrot to say "pretty boy" and "hello," but it would be a sad day indeed if all parrots were confined to such mundane unimaginative expressions. There was a brief news story some time back about a Scarlet Macaw which had escaped. There would be no difficulty in identifying that particular scoundrel, for it was fond of saying "Hello, I'm a red chicken." We have taught our Selsa to say "Here kitty, kitty, kitty". . .and then to answer herself with a "Meow." She also says "Quack, Quack, I'm a duck" and similar other absurdities. Of course, not all her expressions are colorful and like other parrots she has the usual vocabulary of mundane and trite expressions.

While there are considerable disadvantages to commercial recordings, modern technology in teaching a parrot to talk can be put to good use. There are relatively inexpensive cassette players which can be effectively employed in taping one word onto a 30 or 45 minute cassette. Taping one's own lesson plans has obvious distinct advantages.

Imagination can be used in choosing a vocabulary which will be unique to one's parrot. Lessons can be planned to meet the bird's ability and learning pace. One word at a time can be recorded with sufficient repetition to have an impact on the bird. Degrees of difficulty can be introduced as the parrot learns to master one syllable words, then two syllables, and then multi-syllabic expressions.

Self-taping also has the distinctive advantage of utilizing the voice of a master to which the parrot has taken a preference. Most parrots develop a preference for a particular family member, and, when such a preference has developed, it is best to use that person's voice in the taping because the bird will be more apt to imitate the sounds of someone it likes.

The primary disadvantage to self-taped lessons is that obviously someone must actually sit down and for half an hour or more repeat a given word countless times until the lesson tape is completed. A hopelessly boring task! But, once the lesson is finally taped, there is no further exerted effort required until the bird begins trying to imitate the word.

In taping, a child's voice is best because it is flexible and higher pitched than most adults. Unfortunately, it is sometimes difficult to persuade a child to sit before a microphone for any length of time. Failing a child, a woman's voice is preferable because it has a softer tonality than a man's. Most adult male voices tend to be too deep and harsh and since the parrot imitates what it hears, the mimicked sound will also prove to be deep and harsh sounding.

When recording the first lesson, it is best to choose a one syllabled word such as "Hi," as much as the word may seem mundane and common. The hardest part of a parrot's talking lessons is during the learning of the first two or three words when it must learn to imitate sounds foreign to its experience. Once the parrot has gotten the idea that the repeated expression is a sound which it should try to imitate, it will do so. Then the words and expres-

Yellow Naped Amazons *(Amazona ochrocephala auropalliata)* and Mexican Double Yellow Heads *(Amazona ochrocephala oratrix)* are two subspecies which are extremely popular as pets because of their ability to mimic with clarity.

sions can be made more imaginative and complex. But until that time, the lessons should be made as easy as possible for the bird. When taping a lesson, there should be no exaggeration of pitch or inflection, and the word should not be drawn out. Since loud sounds have a tendency to stimulate vocal activities in most birds, it would be best to repeat the word in a louder tone of voice than normally used in everyday conversation. In preparing our own tapes, we like to repeat the word every five to six seconds.

As a final note, when preparing the tape it is wise to have the tape free of various noises which can detract the student from the task at hand. Sometimes a parrot will associate the word to be learned with a particular sound that may be on the tape or occurring somehow during the daily lessons. The parrot then learns to say the word only when that particular distraction occurs in the house. It would sound somewhat foolish for a parrot to say "I love you" everytime the toilet flushed.

A second way of teaching the parrot to talk is for the master to repeat the word or phrase over and over again during each training session. This method has several distinct advantages over pre-recorded devices because the bird is held in the hand during the lessons when it is spoken to. The parrot can focus its attention on the lips, hear the sound directly near its ear, and no doubt even feel the vibrations of the voice. When the parrot's attention wanders, the teacher can force the bird to attend to the lesson. And just as importantly, in using this method the trainer can use the lesson as a vehicle to strengthen his relationship with his pet.

The primary disadvantage with this method is that not only does the voice become fatigued, but a great deal of patience and perseverance is required. For most people, five minutes of boring repetition can seem like an endless ordeal, and if a parrot learns slowly, the teacher may finally give up all lessons because there are no overt signs of immediate progress in exchange for what appears to be a great deal of expended effort.

A final note on methods and content. Some people think that it is 'cute' to teach a parrot various vulgarities. While it may be amusing to hear a parrot say "Who the hell are you," it is a far different matter when a parrot is taught foul-mouthed expressions guaranteed to offend a great many people. A foul-mouthed bird soon alienates many visitors to one's home. The owner is finally obliged to sell the parrot because of this alienation and embarrassment which eventually becomes his lot. Another bird fancier buys that parrot because he finds the vulgarity amusing and because 'the parrot will be the hit of the party.' But there too the alienation and embarrassment eventually come to haunt the new owner. And a perfectly good parrot, one which stands out among his fellows, one which shows a propensity to learn, is ruined because there is no place that bird can remain for any length of time without eventually being evicted. A wonderful creature which could be an endless source of delight and entertainment is reduced to a foul-mouthed vulgarity whom nobody really wants.

This is animal abuse of the worst kind.

THE TRAINING SESSION

Regardless of the method decided upon, the lessons should be conducted on a daily basis regularly at the same time each day. In our particular household, we play our tapes every morning between eight and nine o'clock and again in the evening half an hour after we retire for the night. During both those periods the home is free from activity and sounds which can distract the birds from their lessons. Besides, those times of day are the only hours when we are either out of the house or sleeping—an important consideration since the constant repetition is enough to shatter our pretensions of being sane.

Some trainers prefer to sprinkle the day with several mini-lessons, but our feeling is that by doing so the increased repetition becomes such a common sound in the house that it may no longer command the bird's interest and attention. The only time we do increase the frequency of repetition, however, is when the parrot begins to show signs of attempting to imitate the word. Since his interest in mastering the word motivates him to greater efforts, increased frequency of repetition serves both as a model for accuracy and for even greater efforts on his part.

The problem of distraction is an important problem which must be considered, particularly during the first stages of the training. A parrot's attention span is quite limited, as many of the readers have already discovered in taming their pet and teaching it tricks. The parrot's interest soon wanders to other things and other objects. The bustle about a house can distract the parrot from its lesson. A washing machine may incite a parrot to fits of squawking thereby subverting the tape's effectiveness. A parrot whose head is being scratched or whose wing pit is caressed is more apt to fall asleep than attempt to mimic the lesson content.

Because household distractions are detrimental to talking lessons, many trainers attempt to seclude the parrot from such distractions by covering the cage during the lesson period. In the meantime, of course, family members go about their usual business in the usual way. Kids fight, the television blares, and so on. While the parrot is secreted from seeing things, it is by no means secluded from sounds. Our experience has been that during such times when its cage was covered and bedlam continued as usual, the parrot would invariably decide to contribute his own five cents worth of noise to the confusion. And, if we covered the cage with heavy blankets to muffle sounds, the darkness in the cage resulted more often than not in a sleeping bird.

If it proves to be difficult to maintain the room free of distractions during those periods of the day when lessons are scheduled, then it is best to remove the bird from the room to a more favorable environment. We have even enclosed our parrots in both lighted and dark closets. It works.

In this regard, incidentally, it is wise to remove toys and food dishes from the cage during the talking lessons. A parrot interested in filling its stomach or engaged in demolishing a toy is also generally a poor candidate for vocabulary development.

Regardless of the type of method used, at some point during the training the parrot will begin making sounds which are different from the usual kinds it makes. All birds have their own unique squawks and chirps common to their species. The new sound will depart from its usual repertoire of gobbledy-gook. But the new noises will rarely sound exactly like the word that is supposed to be imitated. A "Hello" may sound like an "O." A "Quack, Quack, I'm a duck" may sound like "uck." (This actually happened with Selsa.) While the attempt to imitate generally takes place during the lesson, the parrot's first attempt to imitate the desired word may take place at any time. The trainer should always be attentive to the sounds that the bird is making, for by doing so he will be able to quickly recognize departures from the usual repertoire.

As soon as it is noticed that the parrot is beginning to attempt imitation, efforts should be intensified. If a recording device is being used, the length of the daily lessons should be extended. If there is sufficient free time in one's daily schedule and the master has a good working relationship with the bird, further use of the mechanical lessons should be avoided and the training should center around a live voice.

The parrot should be taken from its cage, perched on a hand or arm, and spoken to as frequently as possible during the lesson. When you enter the room, on every occasion, the expression should be repeated to the parrot.

Once the parrot begins imitating, it will continue imitating until it has mastered the appropriate sound, if the lessons are kept up. The first imitations will be faulty and so it is important that the expression be repeated sufficiently until mastered. Sometimes a parrot will learn an incorrect pronunciation and it may take several months before the error is finally overcome. When Old

When teaching a parrot to talk, it helps to have the bird porched on the arm.

Blue was taught to say "Hi there," he decided to settle on "Hi Dere." While he was promoted to new lessons in the meantime, the correct pronunciation was repeated to him on every occasion possible until he finally made the appropriate correction.

Once a parrot has begun imitating a word or phrase, it frequently enjoys its new sound so much that it will overuse that word to the point of driving everyone crazy with its constant repetition of its new vocal skill. Parrots like sounds, particularly their own sounds when they are novel. This overkill generally lasts only for a few days, or weeks at the most, until the parrot learns another word which will delight it.

We mentioned Old Blue earlier. He was a somewhat dignified Blue Fronted Amazon who really seemed to have no interest in learning any particular cute expressions we wanted to teach him. Actually, he seemed so aloof from his daily lessons that his disdain was disgusting. We finally gave up on him. One fine summer day we discovered that we had acquired a cricket for a visitor who decided to make our kitchen his home. Every evening around six o'clock or so it would begin its nightly chirping. At first we enjoyed our visitor's singing but tired of it after the second or third day. My efforts to locate and evict him were unsuccessful regardless of how often I moved out the refrigerator and stove. One afternoon about a week after our visitor's unwelcomed arrival, I found him sitting on the living room floor, captured him, and released him outside.

In the meantime, Old Blue had been making odd sounds which was unusual because he preferred dignified silence to bedlam performances. Shortly after the cricket's eviction, an incessant chirping began in the kitchen where Old Blue sat in his cage. When I entered the kitchen, the chirping stopped. Again the appliances were moved without signs of a cricket visitor. This chirping continued for several days and nights, stopping whenever someone entered the kitchen, until we finally discovered that it was Old Blue who was the chirper.

That same Blue Fronted Amazon, incidentally, did turn out to be an average talker. He just happened to be a 'late bloomer' whom we had given up as an impossible candidate for talking, a retarded parrot so to speak. That same parrot had later developed an especial fondness for "O Boy," an expression which he hackneyed to death. He would say it when he was sad, when he was excited, when something traumatic happened to him, and he would mumble it when he was drowsing. Old Blue considered his regular talon clipping a personal catastrophe and when being clipped, while covered with a towel, he would be muttering "O Boy, O Boy, O Boy. . ." Finally, when released from his ordeal, he would really yell it out as he scuttled for the safety found beneath a kitchen table before we found something else that we might do to him. His "O Boy" never failed to be absolutely hilarious during those moments when he suffered personal humiliations, and so we always planned to have his monthly talon trimmings during occasions when we had visitors.

Just as parrots will overkill many of the expressions they have acquired upon first learning them, they will sometimes take a preference to various expressions at their command and complete-

342

ly ignore all the others in their repertoire, even though they may have learned them perfectly. The master should not be disappointed, however, because the parrot is no different from a human being in the sense that it has its own system of likes and dislikes and it exercises its preferences accordingly.

Once a particular expression is mastered, the trainer should begin a new and different lesson. Because a parrot has acquired a vocabulary of a few words or tunes, that is no reason to cease instruction. While it is true that the parrot may now begin learning a few words on its own, such learning will be meager and haphazard at best. If the bird is to become prolific in its command of mimicked sounds, then the lessons must continue on a daily basis. Once, however, a few words are mastered, the teacher will be delighted to find that the parrot's pace at mastering new expressions will accelerate.

Because its rate of learning will accelerate once a parrot has mastered a few expressions, it is at this time that the trainer may wish to teach the parrot to answer a question such as "What's your name." The parrot must first be taught the answer. It is best to use one's voice in this procedure and train the bird during one very specific time of the day each day. Unlike the other type of mimicked expressions, we do not want the parrot to repeat its name at random: we only want it to be mimicked in response to the question "What's your name."

Sit with the parrot fifteen or so minutes each day, say at eight o'clock in the evening for example, and repeat its name until the parrot begins attempting to imitate the sound. Once the parrot begins to attempt imitation, it is best to remove the food dish in preparation for the next lesson. The parrot should be hungry because we are planning to teach the bird a conditioned response. Since the bird now learns quickly, there will probably not be too many lessons involved. As soon as the parrot begins to imitate the voice, give it an "Okay" and reward it. This will encourage the bird to try harder.

Once the parrot has learned to satisfactorily mimic its name, ask the question "What's Your Name," and reward the parrot with an Okay and a tidbit only when it answers with its name. Since the parrot will be stimulated to vocal activity by the sound of your

Parrots of mixed sizes rarely have difficulty getting along well together. More frequently than not, they develop strong attachments for each other.

voice, there is a very good chance that the bird will say something, although it may not necessarily be its name. As the parrot begins to associate its name, however, with the question, the response will become fixed with practice into its repertoire.

Once the parrot answers the question regularly during its eight o'clock lessons, the behavior should be transferred to any time of the day under all circumstances. Every time you enter the room, ask the question and reward with an "Okay" and a treat when the correct response is given to the question. If the parrot volunteers its name, do not reward. In asking the question, vary the distance between the self and the bird so that the parrot will learn to answer the question regardless of whether it is perched on the master's arm or twenty feet away from him. A two or three second delay when crossing the room to give the bird its reward will not harm the mastery of the trick.

Finally we are brought to the last and final point in this section. Should the parrot not seem to learn anything after a month or two of daily lessons, the owner should not despair and assume the bird incapable of learning to talk—particularly if the parrot is from a species with a reputation for talking. Some parrots, like Old Blue, need more time to prove themselves.

If the parrot is not learning, the lesson and its presentation may need to be re-examined. Perhaps there is something detrimental in the entire process which interferes with learning. Is the word simple? One syllable? Are there distractions during the learning sessions? Have the lessons been conducted regularly and at the scheduled time?

Does the trainer during live voice sessions have a good working relationship with the parrot? Is the live voice presenting a clear enunciation? Is the tape clearly enunciating? Perhaps another person's voice on the tape would be better. If a live voice is used, perhaps the presence of the trainer is a distraction in itself and a mechanical device should be used instead. If a tape has been employed, perhaps a live voice and interaction between parrot and master will solve the problem.

The master should re-examine the entire learning environment and institute necessary changes. Sometimes the change can be as simple as a change in the word offered the parrot. And that change can make all the difference in the world.

By all means, be persistent. That is a chief ingredient.

INDEX

Page numbers in parentheses refer to illustrations.

347